TAKE BACK THE MONEY

"OF, BY, AND FOR…"

By   William A. Ward

TAKE BACK THE MONEY

"OF, BY, AND FOR…"

First Edition

Published November 1, 2010
Library of Congress LCCN 2010916044
Self Published Chicago, IL
ISBN 1456305786
EAN – 13: 9781456305789
Printed in the United States of America
………………………………………………

Etch-a-Sketch trademark of The Ohio Art Company

Rorschach trademark of Verlag Hans Huber, Hogrefe AG, Bern, Switzerland

………………………………………………

Special thanks to Dennis C. King for safely leading the way through all aspects of the digital gauntlet.

………………………………………………

The attached copy of the US Constitution was sourced from The National Archives and Records Administration

………………………………………………

Twitter (occasionally):

takebacktheomony   (Note: no "e" in money)

TAKE BACK THE MONEY

"OF, BY, AND FOR..."

THOMAS PAINE: "Perhaps the sentiments contained in the following pages, are not *yet* sufficiently fashionable to procure them general favor; a long habit of not thinking a thing *wrong*, gives it a superficial appearance of being *right*, and raises at first a formidable outcry in defence of custom". Thus Thomas Paine wrote his first sentence to Common Sense. The year was 1776.

There are some very good men in our government. And there are some not inclined to do wrong. But the American people need men and women of principle, those who will place the public good before their personal benefit. In times of stress and at risk to their own physical well-being, those that do so have the hearts and character such that we call them patriots. In the present time, we need those with the same such conviction, a conviction to take a stand and be heard. Nothing short will suffice.

Our country is now deep in debt, and debts eventually come due. And at the time that they come due, debts are either paid, or they are not paid. But if it is *a nation* that does not pay its debts, its status in the world diminishes, and its ability to keep its citizens safe diminishes, and its ability to keep its interests and its cherished beliefs safe, diminishes. Outside its borders, that nation is compromised. And if a nation does not pay its debts, then within its borders, those who have carefully saved their money see the value of that savings diminished, since eventually they find costs skyrocket as the government inflates its currency while their savings are fixed and no longer adequate.

Debts eventually come due. The 2008 financial meltdown was the shot across the bow warning us to get our house in order. The next time it will be a torpedo mid-ship.

One hundred years ago the United States was a robust country. Debt was nearly non-existent; there was little personal debt, and the government debt was miniscule. Obligations for future payment, pensions and guarantees, were nearly non-existent. Debt per citizen now stands at over $43,000 for every man, woman and child, and over $350,000 each if you include all payments obligated by law. Did you know that if you have a family of four, that somehow you are going to bear responsibility for about $1,400,000? We are already seeing the effects of this debt. Our position as a nation in the world is substantially

4

different than it had been previously. Other nations do not necessarily follow our lead as they once did.

At one time this nation was the epitome of wealth and rational society, with the best and brightest the world round coming here, and in doing so they added to the richness of our experience, culturally, materially and in the character of our people. The French were moved to give us the Statue of Liberty, and the great Czech composer Antonin Dvorak came here and wrote his stirring symphonic masterpiece "From the New World", and industrious people scraped together what they could to come here to start a new life, a life of opportunity and productive purpose. Now we find ourselves scolded by other nations for our profligate ways, and from time to time ignored when we wish to discuss matters of vital concern. At one time only one spouse worked and that was sufficient to support one's family. Then both spouses worked and that was sufficient. Now, for most families, both spouses work, and in recent years even that hasn't been sufficient. So people have been making due using the proceeds obtained by refinancing their homes, at least until the real estate crash occurred. Now many have lost their jobs, their insurance and their homes, and in some cases, their families.

Our country has changed, and although the heart is still ticking, the dagger is close to the heart. In some ways we are at war with ourselves, the states fighting one another, ethnic and class politics, stirred up by the politicians, are rampant, and the political parties in Washington are setting the tone with partisan politics as shrill as at any time in memory. The sense of unsatisfied need stoked by our politicians has diminished our belief in ourselves, it has diminished our belief that we are in a national enterprise of shared sacrifice but assured well-being. The politicians in Washington now have much of the national economy flowing through their hands, and to explain the failure of their management of the national economy they stoke animosities as between Americans differently situated and toward those corporations we use to harness and organize our productive labors.

IS OUR GOVERNMENT FUNCTIONING?

We train our politicians that money is the core issue of the nation. From their first political race they find out about fundraising, and about the contributors who believe in them as candidates, but these are the same contributors who also argue for funds and who argue for laws favorable for the causes they champion. For a career politician to work up the governmental ladder to higher offices, that same message is ingrained every day, year after year. At the national level, the effects of the laws requested are enormous, the amounts of money are huge, and those making claims are numerous. This is the job of the politician, day after day, year after year. This is their job description, to deal with those demands, and to keep an eye on their own future employment pending the results of the next election. And if they are able to capture a committee chairmanship, then the track record shows they have even more money to pass out. And yet they worry whether they will have the sufficient funds to be successful in that next election, to "get their message out". The money machine has always been a 365 day a year effort, but now with never-ever-to-stop campaigning, the pursuit of money, along with its alter identity, media positioning, have become all consuming.

The late Speaker of the House Thomas "Tip" O'Neill once famously made the statement that "All politics is local". In one sense he was right, that the people who elect you as a politician live in your district or in your state, and that it is those people you must satisfy to get reelected. It is also a mindset that means that as a politician your constituents must feel you have not only represented their interests, but that you have brought back to the district or state your share of the federal money and benefits. This is true, even though your constitutional duty is to the nation.

The politicians in Washington now bring back money to their districts for anything and everything imaginable. And of course, with every dollar brought back to the district, there is someone else in that district who might also have a claim, so competing interests are split apart and differentiated and multiply, and new rationale are created for yet another claim on the federal treasury. And there seems to be a mindset that the money comes from some vast pool far away, and even if borrowed, well borrowing has been taking place for a long time without consequence, so that must be ok too. It's just the way we do business in America. The funds come from a distant federal government, a government that always seems to have money, and to the average citizen the amounts are so great, they must be infinite at the source. So now our politicians, while attending to large matters of national importance, also spend their time and emotions on things such as placing taxes on airline baggage fees, a serious leak in the federal tax collecting scheme if no tax is imposed.

OUR NATION IS WOUNDED

As we know, the monetarization of our system of government has gone much further. Our states are now under financial siege, in varying degrees due to their own fault or just lack of foresight, but also due to "unfunded mandates", that wonderful device from Washington DC that requires states to spend their own state treasury funds to achieve federal governmental and political purposes. That won't close the budget gap in Washington, but it will at least help conceal its magnitude from the voters. It requires officials at the state level to be the ones losing sleep at night wrestling with the enormous funding issues. The new healthcare act is example number one with its expansion of Medicare costs to be borne by the states. Now the federal government is extending this idea to private individuals, making one private citizen deliver his money to another in the form of a health insurance representative, to the tune of a trillion dollars over the next ten years. Why go through the trouble to try to collect taxes then pay those tax dollars out, when you can have them delivered directly where you want them to go? At first the mandated payments for healthcare were not a "tax" in the eyes of the government, but now they say it is a tax. Credit the government for at least the efficiency to be obtained with the direct delivery of the funds, although the government seems to be budgeting for an enormous number of IRS inspectors to see whether the common citizens have done what they have been commanded to do. So much for the idea of private property, if the government has the ability to direct what happens to it. In the words of Chief Justice John Marshall,

"The power to tax involves the power to destroy".

Add to that that, when urged by a politician, the IRS can be used to stifle political expression or intimidate opponents. Of course one solution is to get a job in the Presidential cabinet, where a full 20% of them are tax cheats. The Pennsylvania Avenue socialists, or at least some of them, apparently have exempted themselves from portions of that tax burden. The integrity of principle they bring to their government service is as certain as the appearance of a chameleon, at least when the polls are at stake or the media is nearby. They are economically expropriating entire industries through legislative strangulation and fiat, being exceeded recently in the brazenness of their actions only by Hugo Chavez of Venezuela.

INVEST YOUR MONEY HERE?

The government is now demanding much of your money, and it promises that your future will be better as a result of their stewardship and wisdom. But do you trust the federal government with your money? Would you let the federal government be your personal financial advisor?

Let's say you could go down the street to a small federal government office and at your appointed time you pull up a chair in front of Mr. Fed Govt, who will be your personal representative after you open up an account. Being cautious about to whom you entrust your money, you ask questions. "How are your investment results Mr. Govt"? Ignore the chart showing that Fort Knox is no longer relevant, and that the government debt is headed to the stratosphere. Don't wince when you are given reassuring words and are told that the government is competent and is turning things around in a tough situation. Ignore the long term chart that shows much the same dismal results over the last few decades, but now accelerating to the downside for the 2010 decade.

Most of us exercise ordinary prudence, and will expect the same of those to whom we entrust our money, so don't we expect the same from the government? Most of us depend on predictability and a conservative and cautious approach to our future welfare, making the effort to plan for our expected costs, our retirement, and hoping to leave something to our families. Unfortunately those in charge of maintaining those standards for the federal government - if it were your investment firm - avoid dealing with the future of this country's financial well-being when it's politically uncomfortable to do so, and when the long term consequences can be kept out of view of the voters, and instead they gear their efforts to short-term political appeasement. They even explicitly decided to "roll the dice" on social engineering in the housing market that helped cause this deep world-wide recession. Whether well intended or not, it did not serve the purpose of increasing home ownership as intended, as laudable as that purpose may be, but in fact destroyed many of those it intended to help. But more to the point, would any actual bank base their policies on a "roll of the dice"? The whole notion runs counter to the idea of prudence for someone being entrusted with your future security and well being.

What are the assurances that that conduct won't happen again? Has there been an investigation? Has someone stepped forward to take responsibility? All that we see in response to this question is finger pointing, finger pointing away from those who engineered the collapse (since they are still in government or are prominent in positions outside of government) no one saying that, yes, they were the responsible party. The government promises to watch over, to regulate and to oversee industries and the economy, so that these results don't occur, so if they are to be believed and the taxpayers are to be assured, why didn't they get the job done? They had then and have now all the necessary resources and authority to do the job, and yet they were and continue to be distracted since what really motivates them is something else, and that is obtaining those extra votes for the upcoming election. So what the American people get instead are platitudes and promises that are not worth the investment of time required to watch on television. We get reassuring words. They'll do better. Things will be different in the future. To bolster the impression media consultants are brought in, and we are treated to Potemkin Village-staged town hall meetings, soft questions from a fawning crowd, vetted ahead of time for proper loyalty.

Other considerations we have when entrusting our money with another person or a firm include their "independence", the ability of that person or firm to not be in a position to let their judgment be clouded by donors or others who hold that politician's interest to a greater degree than those of the citizens, so that their judgment is not clouded by their own self interest. Altruism in favor of the interests of the nation is the standard to which we hold those we vote into office to represent us.

And we should be able to expect at least basic integrity from our representatives in the control of the national purse, being forthright and open with the taxpayers. Earmarks or campaign contribution favors returned do not represent the best of the American system of government, and to the extent these practices fall short they must be condemned. But for some in Washington the honest belief is that earmarks and campaign contributions "with favor returned" are "ok", and if "ok", then there is no harm and no foul. Directing tax deductible foundation contributions annually to provide scholarships for your grandchildren, and letting the taxpayers make up the difference to the Treasury, is not cleansed by a claim of innocent mistake. Finding transparency, honesty and openness is going to be very difficult indeed, in the face of off-balance sheet financing, unfunded liabilities, guarantees that operate as certain future obligations, and deception as to true costs of programs - at least as may be expected in light of the past track record. Based upon this past performance and with no realistic expectation of a change in future performance, the question remains. If the government did not take your money away from you but you could chose to leave your money with the government as if it were an investment advisor, would you do so?

YES, THEY ARE INTOXICATED

Our government debt is expanding at alarming rates, and the government knows it. Nevertheless, as if they are permitted a binge before certain death, the government of the United States of America continues to defy the clear and looming danger that even common citizens are worried about - and economists bluntly warn about. The leaders in this country have arrived at the point where they don't just think in terms of money and more money and the power that comes with it; they now have a vested interest in keeping this routine in place. Socialist largesse, power, influence, personal employment, and a needy public are dictating this path, and it is a path that is well tended indeed. It is not that as though the politicians don't know the difference between what's good for the nation, and its individual citizens constituting the body politic, on the one hand, and what is in their own self-interest as well as that of their parties and their constituencies, on the other hand; it's simply that they chose to benefit the latter as the initial and primary focus. The political cynicism in Washington is unprecedented, profound, and stunning in scope.

So the question becomes whether governmental purposes and objectives are, or should be, anything more than those purposes and objectives derived from raw political consideration. Our Constitution is silent as to political parties; the purposes and functions of those in office are specified within the larger context and purposes of the Nation. As written, the President, Senators and Representatives have duties to the nation, and that is where you will find their job descriptions. Serving the interests of one political party or another, or even their own interests, is not mentioned. But have we not travelled even further away from the obvious purposes these "public servants" are duty-bound to serve? Is it not even beyond politics that now consumes their attention? Is it not, in some cases, just raw power and monetary reward, a game of achievement under the "rules" of the game? Is this an environment conducive to principled conduct and integrity of thought? Is it any wonder the Speaker of the House provided a response sneering at the constitution when asked if there was constitutional authority for the healthcare mandate? She isn't the only member of congress to sneer openly and on camera at the constitution, smug and secure in their arbitrary and wonton exercise of power. Maybe they think that, other than the elections, all power in the nation gets divided between the two main parties, to the exclusion of the people and to the exclusion of the states. If that's what they think, they are wrong.

SO MUCH FOR CHECKS AND BALANCES

The amount of money flowing into and out of Washington has now de facto obliterated, in any meaningful sense, our system of federalism. The states are now simple administrative units of the federal government, sapped of their original role and powerless in their plight. Our system of federalism was founded on broad experience, experience with a dangerous accumulation of power in a central government, and an experience such that the colonists were willing to shed their blood and give their lives to escape its yoke. Yet now that memory has receded into the distant past, as the sprinkling of dollars has softened that vigilance and rendered the public inattentive. The accumulation and control of money has now created a dangerous degree of power and arrogance in our government, and produced contempt for our citizens. Instead of a belief in the creativity, energy and industry of our citizens, the government policies belie a belief in stagnant resources, and that the accumulation of those resources by those more successful in our society cannot possibly be the result of that person's contributions of effort and creativity, but the result of favoritism and the taking advantage of others. Without a belief that the efforts of its citizens are only real solution to the many problems facing the nation, the government has no qualms intruding itself into both real problems and politically created problems, problems it will only make worse. The government then follows up by adding to its meddling and incompetence the yoke of higher and higher taxes on the citizens.

The government is now of the belief that, irrespective of the will of the people, that the government will force through whatever agenda it might have in mind, and will do so with disregard of the damage it will cause. It is the audacity of arrogant ambition. The spectacle of the health care bill travesty, as unachievable and fanciful as is promised goals are, trampling not only on the financial well-being of the country but also subjecting the belief that life should be cherished held true by the people of this nation, to the cost-benefit analysis of distant bureaucrats, has stunned and turned upside down our historic belief in the service of the government being for the people, and not the other way around. And seeing the members of the president's own party walk the political plank - these events now expose the extent that political leverage bordering on extortion has become a tool of a government that believes only in itself. This is an exercise of power, not of authority, because it is not based on principles and is not based on the consent of the governed. The vindictiveness our government has shown toward the exercise of constitutional authority in the country of Honduras, the threat of our Secretary of Health and Human Services for health insurance companies to comply with a non-existent section of the new health bill, the stifling of information from those companies to the public explaining the government mandated cost inflation that's boosting policy premiums, the announced pre-ordained (but now uncertain) results of the now criminal trials in our civilian court system promised by the attorney general, to establish the fairness of our proceedings against terrorists, the attempts to intimidate, suppress and sequester the media and freedom of political speech, the pre-ordained demonizing and rush to judgment to direct to others the fault for its own inept governance, using the veneer of bald but unsubstantiated claim of regulatory authority to by-pass congress, - all display an attitude of power inconsistent with the idea of rule by law. Goldman Sachs, now under attack by the government, rightfully or wrongfully, a firm of immense proportions, as well as Bank of America and Citigroup, two of the largest banks in the country if not the two largest, along with another giant Morgan Stanley, are now showing interest in South Shore Bank, a tiny community bank that's in trouble, that happens to be in the President's old neighborhood in Chicago.

21

Does the idea of Fear of our government come to mind? Are these institutions buying justice, or maybe buying their way out of injustice? Did significant segments of our health industry roll over when they saw the threat a headstrong federal government represented? Are we seeing drilling diminish, not for the environmental reasons, but rather in anticipation of a fickle and capricious government? These are not mere coincidences. Even our philanthropic organizations are starting to toe the line. We are seeing the appointment, sometimes without confirmation, of a new breed of jackboot regulators tasked with the job of imposing new legislative shackles, and who represent a government with the conceit of the few over the wisdom of the many. The economy is in a shambles and all that the government does is distribute money to those who are given access and an audience. The federal government wages a war of attrition against the people of Arizona and their representatives for the extra-constitutional felony of insubordination. Huge sums of money obtained with debts that will be with the nation for many years, are distributed in constantly changing ways as the government tries to re-design its stimulus machine, incubating half-hatched money disbursement schemes based upon economic theories that contain no passion and exclude the people and the stifled energies they wish to unleash. The stimulus is a dose of morphine for the pain of a selected few while the patient continues to get sicker. Politics and the control of the nation's capital resources is a deadly mixture, but you are nevertheless presented with the sorry spectacle of the government propagandists telling you that they are on the right track and that all is well.

GREETINGS FROM GEORGE ORWELL

Our government is now seeking, and is well along toward its goal, to commanding near plenary power over our country and our lives. We have come a long way from the time when under the Constitution rights were reserved to individuals and states under the reservations clause; laws, taxes and regulations now attempt to tie up all aspects of life. Until the advent of computers, the regulations and taxes were as so many Lilliputians trying to tie up Gulliver, but they were limited in their scope and effectiveness. Now there can be myriad strings tying you to the ground, and each one, if not satisfied in a some remote database of compliance, can trigger other repercussions, and all so efficiently done at no cost to the government, no human intervention needed thank you. By one estimate the cost of complying with Washington's regulatory requirements is $1.75 trillion annually. And in the so called financial reform bill that avoids real reform, there is a demand that American businesses report to the government almost all transactions of even marginal significance. As to the personal lives of our citizens, originally the government had the power of conscription to raise armies, the power to take a census and form juries implying some cooperation being required of citizens to be counted and to participate in trials, and later, with the passage of the 16th Amendment, the power to compel the reporting of income and the payment of an income tax. The government now extends that power to compel individuals to do as it commands in any matter it deems to affect the economy. Is there any aspect of your life that does not affect the economy? Do you wear out your mattress at night a week sooner than your neighbor, due to your weight, or the number of times that your roll over in your sleep? Does this not affect the mattress industry? In that case the government has the right to try to regulate your sleep as it affects interstate commerce. In the contemplation of our government, the ends they seek, for whatever motives, justify the means they use. And what is a mandate anyway, if not tyranny? What is tyranny, if not a mandate? Between the citizens and our government, who should be mandating whom? The disregard of the Constitutional limits and the vindictive use of federal power are leading to the dissolution of the legal structures that protect us, and citizens and businesses are scurrying around arranging their affairs to avoid the heavy hand of the government.

Our government has now become ideological, irreparably politicized, distant and isolated from the people, the only voices heard being of those who say yes, and our road signs now tell us who we are to appreciate; whatever knowledge the public may be able to contribute is not heard. Although being politically rapacious may earn some appreciation for its Machiavellian effectiveness, the American people do not appreciate seeing their difficulties and plight - as they lose their jobs, homes and savings - being seen as an opportunity, seen as a "serious crisis.. going to waste", to be used for political ends during a crisis when the public has no choice but to trust its government. The American people do not want command-economy solutions, nor do they want any other ideology other than those inherent in the roots of this nation. The American people do not want a return to an "On the Waterfront" atmosphere in their workplace. The people feel alienated from the determination of their own future, and demagoguery and hollow declarations of successful economic management and national governance simply confirm Washington's distance and indifference, and that political fortune comes before the good of the people. Now angry citizens speak of a ruling class, and speak of the establishment of a thugocracy running the country. Photos taken at sharp upward angles at one's chin-line only inspire hope until such time as actions are assessed, and the promise that was made as to the future is now seen to be the first deceit. The

American people want to see actions that belie a leadership dedicated to something more than mere political expediency.

THE 10TH AMENDMENT SPEAKS TO US

As contemplated when the Constitution was adopted, the federal government would only have those specific powers as granted by the Constitution. All powers not transferred by the States to the federal government were left to the States, unless "prohibited" to the states by the Constitution and left to the people.

Amendment X

"The powers not delegated to the United States by the Constitution, nor prohibited by it to the States, are reserved to the States respectively, or to the people."

....

1) The federal government is only granted those powers specified in the Constitution and no others.
2) If a power has not been given specifically to the federal government, the power is retained by the each of the individual states and the people, but the states are prohibited from exercising certain powers as specified in the Constitution.

This retention of power by the states did start with the Constitution, but was a restatement and enlargement of the Articles of Confederation:

"Each state retains *its sovereignty, freedom, and independence, and every power, jurisdiction, and right*, which is not by this Confederation expressly delegated to the United States, in Congress assembled."

THEY WANT IT DONE THEIR WAY

The extortion of campaign money is a well known phenomenon, and especially when an industry is out of favor with the public. People are now furious with banks and Wall Street. Is it a surprise that this is the time campaign contributions are rolling in (or were coming in until the polls soured for the incumbents) and being accepted by the very same politicians acting so disgusted in front of the TV cameras? Off camera they are smiling all the way to the Bank as the rules and regulations affecting those contributors are somehow modified shortly thereafter. "Whatever it takes" is the modus operandi of the government at this time. Cotton farmers may or may not be having more financial stress than the rest of the citizens in this country, but they are used to getting subsidies from Washington to a degree that recently the World Trade Organization ruled the subsidies to be of an unfair trade practice benefiting the industry and harming Brazilian cotton producers. Rather than reduce the subsidies, and thus run the risk of lost voter support, the Undersecretary of State negotiated a deal such that American taxpayers will not only be subsidizing American cotton producers, but Brazilian ones as well. A senate seat saved is the reason to raise glasses for a toast in Washington, D.C. These are your tax dollars at work, at their finest.

LET'S MAKE A DEAL

The dirt is so thick in Washington and has been so for so
long that the public has become resigned to it. Faced with a
violation of law, the response we hear is "It's just politics",
whether it was the health care bill or the attempt to eliminate
competition for a Pennsylvania Senator no longer wanted by the
people of Pennsylvania. Laws are now passed causing
distribution of funds in vast quantities and arguments are made
by circuit court nominees that there is a constitutional right to
these sums, irrespective of the plain meaning of the actual words
in the Constitution. This is the constitution seen as an Etch-a-
Sketch™ screen. Washington is in complete disavowal of
common sense in matters of the budget. It now foists upon the
public its spin on its own latest assault against the nation, using
numbers that not only disregard the actual track record of the
government's history of failure meeting future projections, but
that also constitute straight out deceptive presentations of
information. With certainty there will again be a failure to meet
future projections, with the result that there is in fact, now, an
implicit decision to reduce or eliminate funding for other future
programs that will get squeezed out as a result of the
unaffordable cost of current programs being passed. And all the

while the government is increasing our debt to the point that it is accumulating based both on actual unfunded government needs as well as the spiraling amount of interest expense. In previous years the government was spending away our future income, now it is cannibalizing what's left of our national wealth, if any. Is it Illinois politics in Washington, or is it Washington politics in Illinois? If "it's just politics" means that these practices have been going on for an extended period of time, then the public has "been had", for an extended period of time.

Contributors now use Washington as giant ATM machine, the difference between the one they use and the one you use being about six or seven zero's at the end of the number of dollars being disbursed. It was the great playwright George Bernard Shaw who said "A government with the policy to rob Peter to pay Paul can be assured of the support of Paul". The question is, what's so special about the "special interests" who get your money? As the mid-term vote approaches we see substantial earmark dollars going to contributors and campaign organizers, the taxpayers' money being used to tilt the election. The two main parties are both at fault here. In both cases they extract as much money as possible from you. The only difference is that the Republicans see a point of diminishing returns in their tax collections at a certain level of tax dollars being extracted, and the Democrats don't. It made sense even in ancient Egypt to provide adequate food so the slaves building the pyramids could return to work the next day, and the citizens of this country are being left with enough funds to get by to the next day, at least some of the time. As balm to the taxpayers the government offers the Small Business Jobs Act, another Trojan Horse to get the taxpayer's money.

The government's rhetoric is telling. In arguing to let the tax increases due January 1, 2011 take place for some taxpayers, stopping that increase is not described as letting those people retain their money. The government presumes that those funds already belong to the government, and that if the tax increase were prevented, the government would be "spending" its money by leaving it with those taxpayers. Why are they not honest and just say "The government wants your money and is going to take it away from you"? This is the mind set, that the government owns everything, and that it will dole out money and property rights as it wishes. Where in the constitution does it say that all money and property belongs to the government, other than that amount they deign to allow us?

If, from the more wretched parts of the old world, we look at those which are in an advanced stage of improvement, we still find the greedy hand of government thrusting itself into every corner and crevice of industry, and grasping the spoil of the multitude. Invention is continually exercised, to furnish new pretenses for revenues and taxation. It watches prosperity as its prey and permits none to escape without tribute.

Thomas Paine, Rights of Man, 1791

WASHINGTON GUARDING OUR INTERESTS

The banking crisis of 2008 largely resulted from the un-hinging of certain agreements called credit default swaps between institutional investors owning pools of mortgages on the one hand, and banks and other financial institutions on the other hand who guaranteed those pools of mortgages. The bank or financial institution received a fee, and if a pool of mortgages failed due to a default on those mortgages, the bank or financial institution would have to make good the value of that pool of mortgages, an arrangement similar to insurance. Pools of bad mortgages were created at the command of the government to promote ill-advised housing ownership and were given so called "Triple A" rating by the federal government sanctioned rating companies. In fact after a while the only basis for the value of these pools was the bubbling up of housing market values due to the enticement of profits in the eyes of investors world-wide. Further oversight of these developments by the government was lacking in light of a pacified public. The crash brought all the ills of these toxic assets home to roost, and the federal government essentially stepped in as the bank or financial institution guaranteeing those mortgage pools. That means in the end, the taxpayers of this country are on the hook, the losses to be paid out of current tax revenues, or to be paid out of future tax revenues when the funds borrowed by the government to weather this crisis-by-blunder, indifference and deflection of responsibility, finally must be repaid.

The financial system came close to shredding - and close to overwhelming our bankruptcy system that serves the orderly liquidation or adjustment of the assets and obligations of individuals and entities in our country – and radical measures where necessary to prevent a complete breakdown of commerce at all levels of the economy, from the individual to the retail store to the largest corporations and institutions, all would have been severely affected. The government chose the bail out as the method of choice. But the asset purchases and the governmental guarantees rising into the trillions spawned by this crisis are neither the only nor the largest examples of the taxpayers being on the hook for governmental promises. Things going to the very fabric of our national life, such as social security, are merely governmental promises. The "Social Security Fund" is not actually a fund other than a small balance to pay current checks, since that money has already been loaned to the federal government and spent. SBA loan programs, disaster relief programs, housing guarantees (and in some sense almost the entire housing industry), some utility investments, most pension plans, bank accounts, accounts at stock brokerage firms, and many, many others are all future commitments to open the taxpayers' wallets.

And while many of these guarantees were and still are benign and in some cases useful, at least when times are good and the beneficiaries of those programs are not under stress, when the programs are not managed correctly, we see the damage they can cause. And when some, such as the housing industry, are misused for political purposes, the consequences can be catastrophic. Two decades ago the government sponsored liquidation of a large portion of the savings and loan industry resulting from another real estate asset bubble popping, that one inspired by the income tax code and US government currency manipulations, ended up costing tax payers hundreds of billions of dollars, even before adjusting for inflation. The life support congress used for the industry, prior to the bail-out, was the notion of "regulatory capital", meaning the savings and loan associations to which it applied were underwater with their assets less than their liabilities, so the congress just said in effect, in the eyes of the laws of the United States, you are deemed to have funds that you don't have. That is the ultimate shovel-it-under-the-rug solution, but a tribute to the intellectual creativity and craven character of the government.

PARTY TIME! LET'S DOUBLE-DOWN FOR OUR VOTERS (VOTES)

So the federal government uses more and more debt, oblivious of the future, other than when it needs to grandstand in front of the media now and then when the public shows worry. At the time of the sinking of the Titanic legend has it that someone uttered the expression "Even God can't sink her", and of course we all know what happened after that, hitting an iceberg on her maiden voyage and going down with great loss of life. We now see that same attitude as to the financial condition of our country, with vast amounts of debt accumulating, and accumulating in amounts greater and greater in magnitude compared to our ability to repay them. And all the while our government continues the house of cards, sputtering to life brief and costly economic activity, rigor mortis like, that otherwise would not occur if left to fundamental and sound economic resources and decision making, but would be replaced by a vigorous drive toward prosperity Do not believe the concern about debt now being shown in Washington by the politicians up for re-election; as soon as the elections have taken place, not all but a majority of the politicians will go back to their old ways. In some ways we are now, on a national level, like Enron

40

Corporation before it financially imploded. It was huge; it appeared to be creative and cutting edge, producing wealth for its investors in new and novel ways. It was a bright shining star in the financial firmament, no doubt about it. The only problem is, the profits weren't real. But the stagecraft that provided the illusion of profits was real, and it was superb. We have accomplished poverty levels not seen since 1960 in this country, and the government is managing its debt in the same manner as an adjustable rate mortgage, borrowing short term, throwing the dice and hoping rates don't rise on $5.2 trillion in debt coming due in the next three years.

YOU DON'T REALLY NEED TO KNOW, DO YOU?

So if you look at the federal budget, there are gaps of information, money appearing from nowhere, such as in the new healthcare act. There is mismatching of information as to the sustainability of the program, showing more years of revenue and fewer years of benefits to make the public think it roughly pays for itself. But even that illusion of balance disregards the trillion dollar cost in the form of mandates, and it disregards as well the Medicare doctor's fee hidden each year, but which will cost additional hundreds of billions in real dollars. Is it no wonder that the Medicare actuary predicts that within the next two decades as many as 25% of hospitals, skilled nursing facilities and home health care agencies will be operating at a loss (and presumably will close)? How many doctors will leave the system? Is there an argument that the government just had a lapse of honesty as to healthcare, but is otherwise being above-board with the citizens?

I GUESS IT ISN'T SUPPOSED TO MATTER

For those addicted by substance abuse and whose lives are crippled, there are twelve step programs and other individuals who will help. And there are controls in society, such as law enforcement resources, that steer those into rehab who can't steer themselves to help. Our government is intoxicated with money and power, and there is no twelve step program or law enforcement mechanism to protect society from the damage being done to our financial wherewithal, and to our ability to continue as a beacon of hope and example of principled behavior across the planet. The conduct of our government is changing the way we see ourselves; we now see ourselves as people who are less self sufficient, as people who are unable to care for themselves and their families and creditors at the end of the month. We are starting to exhibit irritation in our commercial affairs and we have a deep distrust of government. We see erosion of our sense of disinterested communal generosity and instead we focus on our own material shortcomings, for some quite real, but for some mere shortfalls in acquisition of the latest products. The attitude of our government to our citizens, as displayed by its actions, has become one wherein we are considered incapable of making decisions for ourselves, and therefore the desires we express can be disregarded. No wonder a CNN poll reported in the Wall Street Journal April 3, 2010 issue disclosed that 56% believe the federal government is so large and powerful that it poses an immediate threat to the rights and freedoms of ordinary citizens.

HOW WE GOT HERE

At the beginning of our republic the drafters of the constitution wrestled with problems they had encountered dealing with conflicts between the various former colonies operating under the Articles of Confederation. One of those problems was determining how to deal with discriminatory trade conduct by one state against another state - just as we might see a claim of unfair trade practices against, let's say, a country in Asia. Of course in the present day consumers can easily purchase items across state lines, and for any state to have discriminatory laws would be foolish to say the least. But at that time, in order to eliminate trade discrimination problems between the states, the framers granted broad power to the federal government to regulate commerce, in essence to create a free-trade zone among the various states. It is that clause of the constitution that is used by the federal government to justify its intrusion into all aspects of American life.

Franklin Delano Roosevelt threatened to "pack the Court", increasing the number of Justices sitting on the Supreme Court with appointees ready to do his bidding. In response to this the Supreme Court buckled and started to grant the President broad power under the Commerce Clause. They did this in spite of the prior interpretations of the extent of that power and in spite of the clear statement of the powers reserved to the States and to individuals in the 9th and 10th Amendments. Additionally, some Justices and nominees for the Court started saying that they would "defer to the political branches of the federal government", and some continue do so still now, meaning that they would not review or challenge what the President wanted. But is this not a complete abdication of their responsibilities to protect the Constitution, since if the President is not subject to review, do we not have the Rule of Man and not the Rule of Law? Maybe the Court can allow broad interpretation for other litigants, or in the case of matters relating to the President's role as Commander in Chief, or in matters pertaining to treaties, but interpretation with respect to the Executive Branch on domestic matters must subject that branch to the limits inherent in the Constitution - without exception. In the words of Thomas Paine *"The Law is King"*.

That use of the commerce clause has led to bolder and bolder actions of the government against the people. At this point the government is now trying to say that non-commerce effects commerce, that by not buying something you are reducing demand for that item, so the government can order you to disburse your savings to another person or business. So if the government, like a thug on the street with a knife at my throat, orders me to take out my wallet, and I do not do so, then that is one less dollar that has moved in "commerce". By the government's rationale, I have affected commerce by causing the absence of that dollar moving in commerce as directed by the government; therefore I am subject to their jurisdiction and punishments. By inserting itself into all aspects of American life, the federal government demonstrates a need for vast sums of money, distributed under this justification or that justification, to every town, for every farm plot, for every tourist greeting facility as you pass from one state to another.

In order to raise the vast sums needed, the federal government needed a funding facility such that the funds held by citizens would end up under control of the federal government, and to that end, and in order to overcome Constitutional objections, the Constitution was amended permitting the income tax. The country had brief prior experience with an income tax during the civil war. Now the United States was becoming first tier industrial power with a presence and reach across the planet, and additional funds were needed.

The income tax has now been with us for about 100 years and has gone through many, many changes. The tax code is amended in minor ways every year and in a major way maybe every other year. Each time, of course, certain taxpayers in the society are favored by special treatment, a subtle way in which the politicians help those they wish to help while the rest of us pay, or the country goes further into debt. So with each change the tax code gets larger and larger, in spite of names Such as "Tax Simplification Act". Although efforts are made to weed out obsolete provisions from time to time, the tax code is a nest of overlapping provisions that are beyond the scope of any human being now alive or ever in the future to understand in all its detail. The recent stepping-down of the Chairman of the House Ways and Means Committee -the tax writing committee for this most complex and arcane of all our laws - was not a result of the complexity of the Internal Revenue Code. The violations alleged leading to his loss of the chairmanship and his current congressional ethics trial were violations of tax code provisions even a first year tax student would have easily understood. He is being charged that he simply didn't pay his tax on all his taxable income.

Upon the bombing of Pearl Harbor inflicting huge and immediate losses on the American military forces in the Pacific theater on December 7, 1941, a Japanese commander, Admiral Isoroku Yamamoto, is reported to have said "I fear all we have done is to awaken a sleeping giant and fill him with a terrible resolve". The American way of life and attendant liberties and freedoms, our promulgation of principles of human dignity and the rights of individuals across the globe, the high standard America has set for all the world to see and admire in the conduct of foreign policy and the interactions of nations and peoples, these are now at risk by this dissipation of our national strength to a greater degree than at any time since December 7, 1941 when our western coast lay defenseless to aggression. There are some who have taken unprincipled advantage of the nation and the political process, to a degree not even contemplated by the current set of "rules of the game", and there are some who have acted in violation of the law. The vetting and removal of those who have taken advantage of the rules out of our nation's political life, and the ferreting out of those who have broken the law, are matters for the ballot box and for the prosecutor's offices, and they should be forcefully addressed in those forums. For now focusing on scoundrels only distracts into partisan bitterness and will not solve the larger problem nor preclude in any substantial sense the continuation of these practices. What is needed is to remove the ability to engage in these practices in the larger sense, and to do so effectively. What we need to do it take away the money. Once again the sleeping giant has been awoken, and that sleeping giant is the American people. *We need to take away the money*.

Our nation is now at risk.

THE CONCENTRATION OF POWER
OUR BROKEN GOVERNMENT

Over a period of time, with the vast amounts of money
that a remote and insulated federal government has so effectively
extracted from the citizens by enforcement of the Internal
Revenue Code, the power in this country has followed the
money and now is concentrated in the hands of those in
Washington. In turn the States have lost the will to challenge the
federal government in the face of monetary inducements to
follow Washington's direction. Leaving the states paupers
softens them to the compliance to Washington's demands in
light of the funds dangled before their needy treasuries. By some
estimates the citizens of this country have seen their purchasing
power increase little or none at all in over 50 years, so while the
rest of the world becomes wealthier in comparison to us, we
watch them pull even and prepare to pass by.

Struggling citizens, of course, also look to where they
might find relief, and they become even more pliable and more
resigned to the dangerous concentration of power in Washington.
Our cherished systems of distribution of power has been
obliterated as between the states and the federal government, and
our system of checks and balances has been has been eroded

between the congress and the President. It is this distribution of power, now ignored, that is the basis of American "Exceptionalism". It survives mostly, but not entirely, in the form of acrimonious partisanship between the two primary political parties. It's a battle for resources and power.

Our nation is now at risk. As foreigners strengthen, we cut back on our military forces, and we relinquish our leadership. We are now indecisive as to what exactly is America's place in the world, some saying it's the end of "Pax Americana", a period of remarkable stability, development, and the spread of human rights and improvements in health and life expectancy across the globe. Our leaders involve themselves in matters that are entirely internal and matters that are without significance to the viability or strength of the nation. So as we languish, others move ahead, and we have degenerated into partisan bickering as our excuse for government, all the while our citizens are under stress. In our hearts we are highly skeptical of the prospects for our future well-being, and we feel as though we have no ability to influence those factors that might obtain that brighter future for us. We are letting our problems fester, and that augers poorly for the future. Crisis, governmental deadlock, filibusters, and more crises are on the national menu for the foreseeable future.

The portfolio of issues into which the federal government has inserted itself is so vast in number, the amounts of money are so huge, that significant legislation that has the ability to profoundly impact American life far into the future goes entirely unread by those voting for it. It takes all their effort and that of their staffs to figure out what positions to take on "home district" and "political base" portions of the legislation, and to be sure that their own appearance in the media is favorable, and that it positions them well for the voting booth at the next election cycle. So with even the larger issues not read and not understood by those voting for them, no wonder a myriad of smaller issues get attached to the bill that in the end will drain the treasury and pervert the political process, by individual members of congress, and then approved unseen, and not challenged, by the other members of congress. I doubt that there is one Senator or one Representative that read the entire financial stimulus bill (1,419 pages) before signing, or read the entire health reform bill (1,990 pages) before signing, or read the entire financial reform bill (2,323 pages) before signing. Placing pork in the bills is what gets them passed, the essential component of congressional decision making. So we have tens of billions each year going to less than worthwhile purposes, not a huge number in federal government terms, but maybe more

53

corrosive and dangerous to our well-being in the corruption of principles of government, and in the distraction, and in some cases straight-out subterfuge, that is required to be foisted on the American people. We satisfy ourselves with a sense of feeling better in our living rooms. There might not be the ability to do so tomorrow if we do not restore leadership in setting high standards of financial responsibility and our ability to believe in ourselves again, and that leadership must be seen in the federal government. Our government needs to be leaner and more focused on the issues that matter, and needs to address those issues, bringing traditional American principles to the resolution of those issues. We cannot afford ossified government at this point, the threats and risks facing us are too great.

A nation under a well regulated government, should permit none to remain uninstructed. It is monarchical and aristocratical government only that requires ignorance for its support.

Thomas Paine, Rights of Man, 1792

At one time there was a statement and belief that "the business of America is business". And while that statement gave short shrift to our culture, our generosity both at home and abroad, our dedication to the rights of man, expressed not only in our documents and beliefs, but in our commitments and in our blood, nevertheless it was from a sense of pride and competency that exuded our self-image as a nation. And while others had little, America had accumulated wealth, enough to easily fund any undertaking in our national interest, and in the right circumstances, to provide for others. Now we borrow from others, and worry about the day they will not lend to us anymore. This is inexcusable and flat-out unacceptable for America. The business of the nation is not politics; the business of the nation is the business that benefits the entirety of the American nation.

Our economic woes are apparent overseas too, such that an axis of those opposed to us (formerly called "enemies") who fight continuing wars against us by proxy and gorilla terrorism, seeking to install themselves in power and to exercise brute power using the pain of the human body as their tool of choice, is forming, fearless in our ineptitude, indecision and our enfeebled state. And while petty dictators have always tried to sustain their prestige by challenging us with the bravado that distance and insignificance provided, knowing we would ignore them, now they are being given credence, respect, and in some cases institutional support by the UN and others. And this is irrespective of the relative good and evil meted out by their hands compared to the advanced nations. Who, other than terrorists, can argue with the principles enunciated in our constitution? The Chairman of the Joint Chiefs of Staff knows that our debt is threatening our national security, and our challengers and enemies know that too.

TAKE A STANCE

We need to reestablish a culture of values and principles, where we have rule by law, and that law being the written law. We need to do this both domestically and externally. If our laws are a not appropriate for the world we now live in, we need to change them. By adhering to the laws as written, and not based upon the hearts and whims of judges when pertaining to the power of the government or expressions of constitutional Rorschach™ visions, we can encourage self-discipline and respect for the law. Externally, the world needs American principles to be in place and to spread, not destroying other cultures, but enhancing all human beings with principles protecting the rights of men. As expensive as that is, it is cheaper than the alternative, a world increasingly difficult and unstable. Just as it was a mistake to think that the so called "business cycle" had finally come to an end, it is a mistake to think that broader world-wide conflict has been eradicated from the earth. Right now we are cutting back on our military procurement, we have gone soft on our overseas commitments, and we are equivocating as to what behavior we find repulsive. Paying protection money to the mob when they come to the door sometimes masquerades as showing the other cheek to those who intend to harm us.

America does have strengths, and they are many and endure. We have high levels of education, although for the future the generations that follow us will need to have an increased interest in math and science. We have an excellent if aging infrastructure of roads, bridges, air, rail, and waterways. We have near uniformity of language and extensive communication facilities. We have a broad spectrum and multitude of institutions of higher learning, and we have a judicial system that, while having faults of speed and cost, nevertheless is sufficiently reliable for comfort in commercial undertakings and protection of individual rights. We have the rich contributions of the heritages of our citizens who found their way here from every place on the globe. Our bureaucracies are largely competent if not always responsive, and are staffed with well-intended personnel. Above all we have our enabling documents, and our history and culture of tolerance for ourselves and others and challenge to oppressors and wrongdoers. We hold ourselves to the highest standards and principles.

THE AMERICAN PEOPLE SAY "NO"

So where are we now? What is our state of being in this present time? Several trends are apparent in American life, starting with the decline in civility we see in our politics and in those who have been affected by politics. Attitudes about race and ethnicity are becoming more caustic, and now we have calls for Americans to boycott other Americans. Americans now accept this into their culture in the television they are watching, and in the great so called "blue-red" divide. Becoming dependent rather than independent, groveling for resources in the form of tax credits tossed at the public as though the public were puppies sitting on command for the first time and getting a dog bone reward, has lessened the sense of generosity and commonality that has been a hallmark of our national life. Now forty-five percent of us receive some kind of payment or benefit from the federal government, and are otherwise dependent on its capacity and willingness to offer some of our money back to us. Americans no longer save, a trend now happily but temporarily suspended, but a trend toward not saving that has been in existence since the early 20th century. The Chinese, although they have both a command type government and a command type economy with a degree of central control to which we have yet to arrive, in some ways are less socialistic than we in the United States. So that when our government needs to borrow, the Chinese people, who must save to survive and who can't rely on their government for entitlement funds, have the money to lend to us. They also are buying our technology from us, and by selling it to them we are cannibalizing our future, but we need the money.

Beyond the polarization of the political viewpoints in this country, the United States might now be characterized as indecisive. Unlike the Parliamentary system of government wherein the ruling party and prime minister might find themselves out of power at any time if they fall out of favor with the populace, the American form of government provides a stable form of chief executive in the office of the President, who loses that office only under the rarest of circumstances and having committed a "high crime or misdemeanor". Nevertheless, with continuous real time campaigning for power and the politicians always cognizant of the TV cameras, we no longer make decisions based upon the clear, well though-out, best interest of the nation. And while we'd all like to enjoy a pristine environment, balancing the claims of a coalition of tunnel-visioned idealistic interest groups or profit driven advocates on either side is not decisive leadership. When the BP Gulf of Mexico oil spill occurred, the government saw clear to permit drilling in shallow gulf water even while temporarily banning deep water drilling permits during a review period to ensure no further spills. Within days after the shallow water drilling ban was lifted, the permission was reversed under the complaint of environmentalists. Whether it should have been permitted or not in the best interests of the nation, in either case the government should have made a clear and well thought out decision, and not succumbed after being beseeched by a portion of the political base. Ignoring the knowledge and experience of those who've worked with the day to day problems of production in favor of the input of critics and academics does not lend itself to anything other than damaging decisions. And falsifying a report of experts, after their review and without their knowledge, such that those experts had to publicly disavow that report, tells us that the damage to our processes of government are far more severe than the damage caused by the oil well explosion. Similarly taking months to make a decision as to a troop surge is not decisive leadership. And the same can be seen in the conduct of our overseas military and foreign policy actions - equivocation so as to not offend those who can steer votes.

We offer our mea culpa to a UN committee for potential citizen inconvenience due to the possibility that someone might be profiled in Arizona while that state attempts to keep its citizens safe, while at the same time the members of that committee that we supplicate our nation to engage in fraudulent elections, torture, suppression of civil liberties, and government sponsored private executions of its citizens. A country in severe strife, a drug based civil war to the south of us, a Mexican investigator being beheaded investigating the killing of an American on the border, such violence spilling across the border that armed guards must accompany cattle weighing station inspectors in New Mexico and drug cartel assassins are assigned to Arizona, and yet the President will not fulfill the most basic Constitutional duty, since there is political gain - meaning votes - to be had by permitting this danger to continue to exist. It is inconceivable that any previous American administration would not aggressively protect our borders, but that is what we face now. The anxiety being felt throughout the country resulting from the federal government ignoring the border could be ended in a relative blink of an eye if the government decided to secure the borders and proceeded to do so. In spite of this anxiety the government is refusing to adequately fund detention facilities for illegal aliens caught in this country such that all but the felons may be released into our midst. Twelve hundred National Guard troops are sent to Arizona, a fraction of the number needed. They are restricted such that they may not apprehend anyone due to a law called the Posse Comitatus Act that prevents soldiers from acting as police within our borders, so instead they will work computers and otherwise will be generally removed from the border. The law easily could be changed, of course, but with potential votes at stake there hasn't been a word suggestion such legislation. Of those entering the country illegally, what is an acceptable percentage as narcotics distributors? This is a matter not just affecting Arizona and the adjoining states. One Senator reports that the drug trade is a $25 Billion industry, that 230 U.S. cities already have a Mexican drug cartel presence, that 90% of the cocaine, 50% of the pot, 50% of the methamphetamine, as well as weapons and possible terrorism motivated individuals, are entering the country this way, some carriers getting caught but bribing their way in anyway, since so much cash is available. Now the government is entertaining various justifications for releasing those people into our society even when caught, ensuring various government protections and benefits, while at the same time explaining that there aren't enough "beds" in which to place these law violators such that they may be processed. We are the country that was able to keep an entire city supplied by air for over a year during the Berlin Blockade, but we apparently don't have the resources to complete the wall we voted to build, nor to properly process those breaking our laws.

Maybe Arizona needed to mention some 212 other nations on the planet and direct its law enforcement officers to look equally for illegals from these other parts of the world entering their state, envisioning equal risk in illegals from Vatican City or the Pacific Ocean nation of Vanuatu as from those crossing its southern border. All Americans are now feeling an erosion of our territorial integrity, where since September 11, 2001 we have not only had several additional terrorism events and terrorist acts just across our southern border, but we now have one-twelfth of the births in the country to illegal mothers, portions of Arizona declared unsafe for citizens, portions of Texas and New Mexico where American citizens get safety warnings or escorts, gunshots from across the border into Texas, home grown jihadists, and attempts to bring Sharia law into enforcement by the courts here, the controversy over the ground zero mosque (the objections to which never would have occurred had it not been for the September 11 attack), and crippled efforts to conduct terrorist trials in

Manhattan. There are those who take advantage of the benefits of American life by crossing over without complying with our laws, and those who derive their political power from that migration into this country. In effect, our government recognizes the border in the abstract only, but does not wish it to exist in real terms. Those twelve hundred troops will provide surveillance and computer related functions, a help certainly, but safety now depends on local law enforcement and vigilantes patrolling the border, as best they can. Our border is treated as if it didn't exist, since there is a political calculus involved. Equivocation, uncertainty, and subterfuge are the earmarks. Our national leadership is entirely ossified, in the most generous interpretation, and in a dangerous world, that is like fighting with your hands and feet tied.

We now watch the government's war on the productive and job creating sector of our society. With our government entertaining the false fantasy that it knows more about business than those in business know, no wonder the economy has stalled out at a painful level such that the government tax revenues are short and countless families and individuals are suffering. Only four out of the top ten companies getting patents in the U.S. in 2009 were U.S. companies, where not too long ago all ten would

65

have been U.S. companies, and our share of high tech exports world-wide has dropped from 21% to 14% in a mere 5 years. We ask ourselves, where did opportunity go, especially for the poor and the middle class, why does the government suppress them? Why does not the government restore the opportunity that existed when the economy reflected the production of the people, not merely the redistributions of our money? Outside sovereign functions government run businesses are the largest and least efficient monopolies of all, and as to sucking the resources from the rest of the economy the government is the mother of all parasites. No wonder the American economy is seriously weakened.

To see the difference between stifling central economic regulation when compared to the vibrancy of an economy when the people are unleashed, just compare the nighttime satellite pictures of South Korea compared to the darkness of North Korea. Statism was tried in Eastern Europe, and failed. The lesson wasn't noticed here.

Call us the radical center if you will. We believe that the centrist vision is the vision of limited government, the vision of our heritage of liberty, prosperity and strong individual character. It is our goal to restore integrity to government and to governmental financing. We need to separate money from governance to the extent it's not needed for sovereign functions. Our number one goal is to restore the rule of law. We need to reduce the Constitutional functions of our federal government to the least number of functions necessary for the preservation of the nation militarily and diplomatically as well as certain limited internal functions that can only be performed at a central government level.

James Madison addressed the functions being given to the federal government and those being retained by the states in the Federalist Papers No. 45:

"The powers delegated by the proposed Constitution to the federal government are few and defined. Those which are to remain in the State governments are numerous and indefinite. The former will be exercised principally on external objects, as war, peace, negotiation, and foreign commerce; with which last the power of taxation will, for the most part, be connected.

The powers reserved to the several States will extend to all the objects which, in the ordinary course of affairs, concern the lives, liberties, and properties of the people, and the internal order, improvement, and prosperity of the State."

Our method is to disburse the money back to the states and the citizens, or more properly let it be retained by the states and the citizens who are its true owners, to reverse the excess concentration of money and power in Washington, and to make our nation immeasurably stronger and enduring in the process. There is an expression "Don't fix it if it isn't broken". The converse of that is, if it is broken, fix it. We intend to fix it.

THE PEOPLE SPEAK

WE RESOLVE to fix America. We call for the
Constitution of the United States of America to be amended in
the following manner for the welfare of the nation and its
citizens:

FIRST, we call for the Revocation of the Commerce Clause of
the Constitution of the United States of America as regards to
regulating commerce between the States. All governmental
functions attributed to laws enacted pursuant to that clause shall,
on, or before the 10th anniversary of the enactment of this
Revocation, be transferred to the States acting in consort. The
laws and regulations existing pursuant to this section shall be
deemed adopted by each of the individual states, until they act
otherwise. Thereafter no state shall enact any tax, law or
regulation pertaining to commerce between the various states,
unless by agreement of all the states or as by other rule adopted
by all the states.

SECOND, we call for the Revocation of the 16th
Amendment permitting the direct collection of income tax from
the individual and corporate citizens of the United States. In its
place the federal government shall collect such revenues as are

properly voted upon by the congress and signed into law by the President directly from the States in proportion to their populations, and shall assess with a priority claim on the State treasuries for collection of the same. No national sale tax, vat tax or other direct tax may be enacted by the federal government, its revenues to be obtained from the states and from those sources other than the income tax from which the federal government currently receives its funds.

THIRD, we call for the number of justices of the Supreme Court of the United States of America, when no vacancies exist, to be set at nine.

FOURTH, we call for the reaffirmation of the clauses reserving those rights that are not specifically given to the federal government to the states and to the Citizens.

HOW THEY TOOK THE MONEY

A brief history of the conditions leading to this proposal is required. Before the country was governed pursuant to the Constitution we now have, the States operated under the Articles of Confederation. At that time each former colony saw itself as a small sovereign nation, jealous of each other and competing with each other, but drawn to each other as a result of their vulnerability and the similarity of their peoples and experiences. So the Articles of Confederation were adopted, joining the former colonies in a treaty-like arrangement. As was previously mentioned, discrimination in commerce from one state to another was a problem, limiting trade between the colonies and limiting the economies of the individual states. The Articles of Confederation were drafted and adopted intentionally to create, not a strong, but a weak central government, as the experience of the colonists with a powerful and insensitive central government in England was all too fresh in their minds. When the common good required something more robust than the Articles of Confederation and the Founding Fathers began drafting the Constitution, they sought to strengthen it in ways they felt necessary but lacking in the Articles of confederation. But the framers still retained a healthy fear of the centralization of power. The Constitution as a result was written with only a specific and narrow delegation of rights and power to the federal government, and by its specific terms all other rights and powers, whether mentioned or not, were retained by the States and the Citizens. The way our federal government has evolved since that time is exactly what the framers feared and tried to protect against, and exactly why the colonies rebelled and sacrificed their blood and their lives. The central government they envisioned had limited internal purposes, delivery of mail, the raising of armies, and so on, but primarily the Constitution that replaced the Articles of Confederation was intended to better protect the joined states against external threats.

The success of the Constitution along with the industry of the people, unimpeded by a distant government, led to the emergence of the United States as a world power as the end of the 19th century approached. Beginning about the time of the spread of the Industrial Revolution in the United States, following the Civil War, greater regulation of the conditions of workers, attempts to control disease epidemics, responses to banking panics, and the emergence of nationalism and unified European nations, where previously there had been a collection of smaller entities, such as in Germany and Italy, all led to a necessity for the United States to centralize its functions as it grew on the world stage. With the Spanish yielding their far-flung holdings to the United States following the Spanish-American War, America emerged as a world power. The utility of a strong central government was apparent, and the collection of revenues by the income tax came to be seen as a generally accepted evil. The subsequent change in our national character and the erosion of our way of life resulting from this concentration of power were masked by the great stresses of the period, the Great Depression, followed by World War II and the Cold War.

Over time this concentration of money and power has transformed our government such that it is now top heavy and broadly expansive in the scope of its undertakings and meddling, incapable of clear decision and attention to those matters ensuring America's historic role as a leading nation. As to limitations on the power of the central government, founding fathers had it right. There are in fact few functions that by their nature can only be performed at the national level; most of them do not need to be performed by our central government. And while strenuous arguments and challenges will be made, for most functions now in the federal sphere, if suggested to move to the states' sphere, the appropriate question to ask will be "Why not?" Elimination of all functions that can in fact be performed at the state level will free the federal government to attend to the matters critical to the strength and survival of our nation and peoples.

THEY WORK FOR US

The American people demand to once again have a national government that meets our ideals. By moving functions to the state level, we can free federal officials to act in our national interest and seek compromise with those in different parties, or with those proposing different solutions to the problems of the nation, so that once again we can have robust but healthy dialogue and debate across the political spectrum. The idea that all commerce has interstate effects and therefore all commerce is within the purview of the federal government needs to be retired to the history books. The dangerous idea that the federal government can mandate the conduct of the citizens of this country needs to be challenged and defeated in the absolute, for it is the antithesis of freedom. The idea as practiced by politicians in this country that the Constitution can be "gamed" must be challenged for what it is, a profound violation of the rule of law and the culture and principles of this country, and the trust of the citizens. Trading a vote on large bills only when they contain a pet provision "bringing home the pork", this practice must be eliminated. It is a distraction and a perversion of the duties of those in national office charged to focus first on the welfare of the nation.

George Washington was a member of no political party, and in fact was disdainful of their purpose, and there were no "earmarks" attached when the framers drafted the Constitution. In the present day the continuing welfare of the nation demands the same level of loyalty, attention and commitment to the issues confronting us on an on-going basis as was given by the framers at the time of the founding of the nation. The idea of using the power of the government against the people, a development just now appearing in our national experience, is entirely abhorrent. And yet recently entire industries have been made to heel at the foot of the federal government upon implicit threats of a directed misuse and abuse of taxing and regulatory powers.

OUR CAPACITIES, OUR CONVICTIONS

Economists make a distinction between what they refer to as the "Nominal" economy and the "Real" economy. So that while most of us think in terms of money, wages, the cost of cars, houses and gasoline, those numbers can not only inflate over time, but they can be and are subject to changes in the relative value of the dollar compared to the currencies of other countries. We can also be distracted into focusing on the wrong issues, so that while we focus on the national debt, as we should, we also have to be mindful of the larger issue, the welfare of the nation as a whole. In that regard it might be easier to think in terms of the "Real" economy.

To explain the real economy, let's say you were a traveler from a distant planet and you were hovering over the earth looking at the conduct of the planet's inhabitants. You would not see the exchange of dollars or other currencies, but what you would see are people going to their jobs, at factories, in schools, in office buildings, and you would see trucks and ships, and tractors being operated on the farms and so on. And in all this activity you would see the movement of material and the provision of services, bringing order, good health, and so on. This is the real economy irrespective of cost and government.

This is the product of our productivity and a display of our consumption. Occasionally this activity is out of balance, as when there is more consumption than production, and in these situations people utilize their savings, or borrow, as needed.

America's ability to produce is still sound, although our economy is suffering fatigue and is unable to compete in certain industries due to labor immobility, the wasting of resources and other government inspired inhibitors. On a national level we now allocate a great deal of our resources out of the productive sector by way of higher taxes and costs, at a time when we need to allocate more and not less to compete internationally, and our nation is being harmed as a result. Borrowing money is not a permanent solution. Because so much of our economy is now transacted through or under the control of our central government, we as individuals have lost the sense of competitive productivity. In some ways America is tired, and some argue that the cause of this national exhaustion is the burdens we have born over the last 70 years, World War II, the Korean War, the cold war, and so on. But in fact if the real economy retained the resources it needed to regenerate itself, not just the crumbs left to it by the government, our vibrant and robust economy and our sense of strength and leadership would rapidly return. Our people need to start believing in themselves again, and in their ability to save and to provide for the future, but having only such material rewards for our labors and creativity as the federal government permits is stifling the American people and our attitudes and motivation. When was the last time government reduced taxes simply to reduce them? In the best of circumstances they are reduced to enhance the economy and the resulting tax collections. There is no reason not to take that reduction as a building block and then reducing taxes even further. There are no examples of that additional tax reduction occurring in recent times, are there?

Now that there is a collapse of demand since the government couldn't artificially inflate the housing market forever, the government is resorting to that Keynesian cadaver of economic theory to try to pump money into an economy while preventing the obvious hunger and desire of the people to propel the nation forward. Even worse, as they government dawdles and Rome burns, they don't even let the people know what the rules of the game will be. The issue is not one of demand, or the supply of money. There is plenty of money, and there is plenty of demand. The people want cars and houses, they want a secure future for themselves and their families, they want to fix up their deteriorating lives. Let's call that real demand. But the economy doesn't work since the near term status of the tax code is uncertain, 533 regulations as well as 67 studies and 94 reports are to be issued pursuant to the new financial regulation bill, the government is menacing the business community with cap and trade and a myriad other threats. No wonder no one is being hired, businesses don't know where there economy is headed. The government has simply created fear and crushed any stomach for risk taking, since the dangers it has created are simply too great. Those about to put "Help Wanted" signs out are on stand-down as the government works to devise the next financial body-blow to administer. Economic activity remains in intensive care and no jobs are being created. Demand needs to be unshackled from the fear of the federal government.

Creating jobs is not a difficult concept. If one day in a depressed region or town a wealthy man or woman showed up and said they had money and know-how, and could put people to work and provide a needed product, if they were welcome they would stay. But if that same man or woman were to be told upon arrival that a heavy tax along with crushing regulation were to be imposed, not to mention regulators adverse to their interests and holding broad discretion to tell them how to run their companies, would that person set up shop and put out the "Hiring" sign? Would you? Politicians treating business owners and corporate leaders (except their corporate campaign donors) as somehow evil to a degree greater than the population as a whole simply has no justification in fact, but the leaders in Washington demagogue and tarnish those job creators and leave the country straining and vulnerable in a bid for their own individual job security. Animus toward business is the best way to make sure that the unemployed stay that way, and that opportunity is rung out of our future. The simple fact of the matter is, when it comes to economics, they have no idea what they are doing. And only those who agree with their stagnant and erroneous ideas are being listened to. Now the Federal Reserve is on the verge of compounding the problem by printing money to fund the federal deficits under a policy known as "QE2". There may be some short term benefit and a few jobs that result from such policy, but other investors in government bonds know that the repayment will come in dollars with less purchasing power and from an even more weakened economy. The Federal Reserve cannot create long term jobs with such a policy, and no business will invest knowing that such a policy will only drag out the period until our economy is once again on a healthy footing. "QE2", quantitative easing round two, is actually QE2D, quantitative easing of discipline and discomfort, a painkiller sought to ease the effects of substantial fiscal mismanagement of the US economy by the federal government.

WE NOW STAND UP

We need to restore the strength of the nation. We need to restore our instinct as a nation to act on principle. We need to restore the vitality of our nation. We need to deter the intrusion of the federal government into all aspects of our lives, as our lack of focus and our distraction, effectuated by a big and distant government, has given the people of sense of helplessness and need. Sacrifice for the better good has been replaced by a wincing over the inconveniences and difficulties of life. Surviving by using credit surely reinforces the sense that one cannot adequately provide for one's self and one's family. We need to see efficiency and economy at the top of our society, in the functioning of our government and in our institutions, and also in ourselves and our families. The wagon trains travelling into uncharted and ungoverned areas of our west a few generations ago did not have a federal government nearby to provide for their needs, nor to take their money. They went anyway, and they provided for themselves, and although society has changed dramatically, we need to rediscover our full capacity as individuals. We need to be confident in our competence and sufficiency, both as to character and as to attitude, in our private lives and on our jobs.

PAX AMERICANA

Overseas we are becoming known, not as the strong and principled country noted for its "exceptionalism", but rather a county declining from that past, one to be paid attention to, but not to the degree as before. There are arguments, but none legitimate, that the world has changed in such a way that American strength and principle and exceptionalism are no longer feasible. These attributes are derived from our character and our unique circumstances and heritage, and they are not dependent on whether the world changes or not. We need to now show the world that we have not lost our way, that we are vibrant and strong, that we are not ossified, indecisive and only marginally relevant. Above all, for the world to see the American people exert constitutional control over our government, to re-affirm and ratify that heritage so admired across the world and feared by despots across the world, to show that even our central government can be made responsive to our will, will restore hope and encourage democratic aspirations everywhere. Take the worst cases, those people suppressed under the regimes in Cuba, Iran, North Korea and so on, who yearn for the simple freedoms we have always had in this country, at least up to the present time. Read about Neda Agha-Soltan who with her countrymen yearned for the freedoms we take for granted here - before she was killed in the streets of Tehran in June of 2009, as the Iranian presidential election results were being falsified. What could be a more powerful expression of democracy than to see the people take away the money that arrogant and ideological leaders need to thrive? The others in the world will be impressed, not just with our freedoms and economic and military might, but by our character, and by our regenerative determination.

THE AMENDMENT PROCESS

Article V of the Constitution provides two ways to initiate the amendment process. In the first instance with two thirds of the house and two thirds of the senate the proposed amendment goes to the states for ratification, and in the second instance two thirds of the states may call for a constitutional convention to propose amendments. Although the second method has never been used, in light of the growing cancer of unfunded mandates and the trampling of the rights of the states as reserved under the tenth amendment, that tool may be taken out of the drawer. This is the sword of Damocles that hangs over the head of those who would rule you.

SO CALLED STRUCTURAL DEFICITS AND
THE NATIONAL DEBT

The term "Structural Deficits" refers to that portion of the federal government's annual spending in excess of its revenues that goes toward payments and services that the public has been trained to expect. Of course there is nothing "structural" about those payments as any law or custom can be changed, so by the term "Structural Deficits" what we really mean are politically indoctrinated expectations and demands. But there are many whose lives are geared toward these payments and services and their continued well-being must be taken into account. Of course if one is owed money and the debtor has nothing to pay that debt, the mere promises and raised expectations aren't going to put food in the stomach at the end of the day. Maybe that is the reason that 60% of our population does not think that Social Security will pay when the time comes for them to retire, and that there is wide-spread belief that Medicare and Medicaid will be pared back and critical services functionally discontinued. So why haven't these programs been fixed? If those in Washington wish to lead the country, why has no one stepped up to bat to fix the problems? Some aspects are subject to easy solution, others may require an adjustment period that will be briefly inconvenient until a better and more secure administrative scheme is functioning. The problems with these social programs have been well known for decades. Solving the problems is a responsibility that has been skirted putting at great risk the elderly and the other enrolled beneficiaries and future beneficiaries. The funds paid into these funds have been spent and there is nothing there to sustain those promises. Where are the future payments going to come from?

The International Monetary Fund has recently issued a report showing the perilous and unsustainable financial direction in which the United States is headed. Their report is not subject to the same deceptive practices that Washington utilizes with its citizens. People now reflect that we are headed in the same direction as Greece, a nation that is in unannounced bankruptcy. The Congressional budget office shows the US debt up to 62% of the economy compared to 40% two years ago, and the situation is only getting worse and in a very short period of time, with the same patterns we are in, will be beyond the point we can meet our obligations even with borrowed money. The Bank of International Settlements, which is the bank that sets standards for central banks like the Federal Reserve, has painted a gloomy picture for many of the developed nations, but a particularly gloomy picture for the United States due to our reckless pattern of spending. Over time, we are cannibalizing our own economy such that our ability to produce goods and services is on the verge of decline.

WHAT ARE WE LEAVING OUR DECENDANTS?

The answer is clear. We are leaving them enormous debts, a diminished capacity to defend our nation and our liberties and freedoms, a scheme of government where citizens are told what to do and there is no restraint upon authority, and a reference in the history books to a time of opportunity and promise.

What is our duty to our descendants, to our children? Is the duty not just as great, or greater, than the duty to ourselves? Can a society affirm its principles and strengths without creating a future for those who come after us, without acting in accordance with those principles?

In the courts, when there is a minor child, let's say a sixth month old child whose parents have been killed in an accident, the court will appoint an attorney or other responsible person to look out for that child's interest, a guardian ad litem. With our society passing onto such innocents such debt and risk, it is unfortunate that there is no one at the voting booths voting for their interests. If there were such a guardian to vote for the children who inherit our debt, you would certainly see a change in the platforms that the parties run on. At some point in the future, will our children then grown look back and ask why we didn't fix these problems while we could, and before they grew? But for now, these innocents don't vote, so they inherit the debt, and they inherit the problems.

SOME PARTICULAR CONCERNS

While we continue to disregard the existence of a border between the United States and Mexico, the violence there has come to the point where it is on occasion being described as an insurgency or narcoinsurgency and transnational in nature, referring the reach of the cartels into the United States. The President and Secretary of State are aware of the situation, the Chairman of the Joint Chiefs of Staff is reported to be increasingly concerned, and our military is following the situation closely.

At the same time on this side of the border, former 9/11 Commission members have now issued a report that says, as reported in the Wall Street Journal, that the terrorists have established "an embryonic terrorist recruitment, radicalization and operational infrastructure" within the United States. The idea for the radicals is that home grown extremists will be able to more easily blend into our culture and evade our watch. Apparently 63 Americans have been charged or convicted for terrorism or related crimes targeting the United States just since 2009.

THE 1930'S DEJA VU

If civilization is not in decline, then it is certainly under a severe challenge. In western countries the great achievements of freedom and liberty are assaulted by fear, uncertainty and indecision. The United States enjoyed the safety of a geographically remote location until the end of the last century, but it doesn't enjoy such safety in this century, nor will it ever again.

We face an enemy of wrathful and messianic torturers and killers, one that takes glee and celebrates in its savage maiming and killing of innocents. But we fear. We fear of our own responses, our own desire to rid ourselves of the problem, knowing that we risk our tradition of first seeking instead humanitarian solutions, and that we risk our freedoms and way of life. We are afraid to offend, and we are simply afraid from a sense of being overwhelmed by sinister events and forces that relentlessly encroach upon our lives. We have no bright lines and easy decisions, and we have now chosen to be defensive and indecisive regarding our principles, instead of assertive. Do we offend Muslims by denying their right to have a Mosque built near Ground Zero, and do we have a sense of loss of control and order in our society if we do? There is no crystal ball perfection in making decisions, but they have to be made, and best made promptly. It is not in our nature to cower, and yet we have forfeited the resources to properly face and restrain the growing threats that face us. We face an enemy that scoffs at the resources we still can bring to bear, as that enemy draws upon the despair of the uneducated masses to make its nihilistic and destructive clarion call for martyrdom. Its goal is raw power, and its means are without soul.

We face a world with eerie parallels to the 1930's, both in the profile of larger economic forces playing being played out and in the decisions being made by governments. Appeasement of tyrants, policies that subdue the masses while at the same time prolong economic failure, protectionism through currency legislation and xenophobic trade affecting policies, substantial voter fraud, the demeaning of political opponents, the promotion of cult like wistfulness toward messianic leaders, and all the while the tinder of international confrontation gets dryer and more dangerous – all these elements are repeating themselves before our eyes. Of course at that time in the 1930s there weren't nuclear weapons nor the frequent occurrence of major terrorist attacks around the globe. Some nations are becoming more authoritarian in response, and some are vacillating. Our first and primary goal of course is to prevent a nuclear device from being used, and it is not reassuring that nuclear proliferation proceeds slowly but relentlessly as it has been since the end of World War 2. Fanaticism, nuclear weapons, funding, communications, wars by proxy under the public opinion radar, ruthless ambition for power, it is an explosive mixture with the finest of hair triggers set to detonate. A branch of Islam, Wahabism, is the gene now resident in the malignant cells within the body of Islam, endangering Islam, and using the shell of religion to keep the west off-balance and on the defensive. Since 9/11 their presence continues to grow, death in their eyes like so many zombies in an old movie, advancing their prescription for a world controlled by Sharia law. We cannot afford to politicize military decisions as to troop levels, especially when extremist forces battled to within sixty miles of the capital of Pakistan last year, a nation possessing nuclear weapons.

Of course Iran has a large part in this. It is now conducting a war against the United States and other countries using its proxy armies, having de-facto annexed Lebanon and is paying a bounty for the killing of American soldiers in Afghanistan just as it provided IEDs to kill Americans in Iraq. It funds much of the frequent carnage that it hopes you will see on your TV screens at the end of the day It has designs to become a regional superpower and mega-state, one that especially suppresses women, and it is now also reaching into South America. China is devoting great resources to have the facility to disrupt the United States militarily, primarily through electronic disruption of our satellites and other defensive capabilities, also known as cyber-warfare, and has made clear its designs on the entire Western Pacific basin by directly challenging out military forces there. Is it time for Japan to rearm? Will that help balance the power within the region if we are not willing or capable to do so? Will there be an imbalance if Japan does not rearm? Is an arms race in the far-east, as there appears to be in an early stage, or an arms race in the mid-east, in our best interest?

The time has passed for well-intended but wishful idealism and now requires a return to principled pragmatism. We need a Teddy Roosevelt-like aggressiveness toward those who now waging war against us in their attempt to prepare the world for a nuclear blaze. We need to face these threats with strength and without fear, since through our strength other nations of strength will join us, and those nations of good heart but who are weak will become stronger, and will join us too.

96

Our enemies have learned how manipulate our television and public opinion, and they know that in a direct war both our military and our public will rise against them. So now we endure war waged indirectly, but with the same objectives, by proxy, and our enemies hold news conferences and plead their cause. We are now suffering the first non-national, post internet war, and the enemy is attempting to find a weakness in our resolve to it to exploit.

We will only be able to disengage when the extremists are killed or imprisoned, and the rest of the fighters and clerics learn to celebrate and cherish life above ideology, and to celebrate and cherish life even above creed; in spite of any doctrine or belief or fatwa, no god or deity would expect less.

We need a fully functioning economy to face these challenges. We need the federal government to be fully focused and engaged for the future well-being of the nation. We need to unleash the potential of our people.

CHANGING NOTHING

The proposal is much more, and at the same time is much less, than meets the eye. Changing the authority over vast amounts of money will clearly change the path that American society is taking. But in another sense, all that will happen is that the most domestic functions now taking place at the federal government will be taking place at the state governments, in many cases the states acting together, with little or no change in the actual functions. There are no suggestions here that change a single dollar of a budget, other than to move commerce clause based programs from the federal government to the states. The vast amount of contact that Americans have with their government is with the bureaucracies such as the IRS, and the functions of those bureaucracies will be taken over by the states, but otherwise remain intact. By re-introducing the role of the states in American life, we can re-introduce the experimentation by the states in ways to improve governmental functioning. In effect, the bureaucrats can re-program their telephone dialers and direct those calls to their respective statehouses instead of to Washington, and some revenue agents and bureaucrats will have to be rehired by their states. The proposal changes nothing other than to reverse the dangerous accumulation of power in

Washington and to protect the judicial branch from political manipulation. This is intended as a first step, not a step to increase or reduce the size of government or the services offered, but a step to dissolve the paralysis that prevents us from fixing the problems. Fixing the problems is step two and it's taken in the statehouses. The issue is not whether there are winners or losers. The issue is not whether there are short-term disparate affects or discomforts, and if any individual is directly affected that impact will be for a short period and minor in degree. The issue is the health of the nation.

YES, THEY ARE MORE THAN CAPABLE

There will be those who argue that the States do not have the expertise that the federal government has, nor that the states will act with anymore disinterested integrity than the federal government does now. The matter of expertise is now muted by the coordination of activities at the state level and across distances due to the internet and modern communications and centralized databases. Again, for each function that is challenged as requiring exclusive federal government responsibility, the question to ask is "Why not? Why not have the states perform that function in a concerted effort?" If it is the launching of satellites or the negotiation of a treaty, the procurement of a new class of submarine or the protection of the capital markets as far as intra-day operation, or the monitoring of banking reserves overnight, there is no question that these functions must be centralized and are essential to the survival of the country, and that the federal government best performs those functions.

Society in every state is a blessing, but government, even in its best state, is but a necessary evil; in its worst state an intolerable one; for when we suffer or are exposed to the same miseries by a government, which we might expect in a country without government, our calamity is heightened by reflecting that we furnish the means by which we suffer.

Thomas Paine, Common Sense, 1776

He also said in The Rights of Man that when citizens lose rights and liberties:

A Nation has at all times an inherent, indefeasible right to abolish that government and establish a new one.

And while it is not necessary, as it was in Paine's time, to "abolish" the government, we are now at the point where that government needs to be reined in and portions of it removed. But we do not start from scratch. At many levels there already is coordination between state governments and there has been for a long time. So for example, when "right turn on red" became the law of the land, it actually represented the passage of 50 identical traffic laws, one by each state, all taking effect on the same day. Your ability to turn right on red is pursuant to state law, not federal. There is an organization sometimes known as the Uniform Law Commission, formally the "The National Conference of Commissioners on Uniform State Laws", that has been in existence since the 1890s, that recommends and coordinates agreements between the states for laws best adopted on a uniform basis across the country. Additionally there are national conferences of governors, and of administrators, at many levels of state government, with different mission statements, but in contact with each other and having organizational structures in place. Fifty Attorneys General are now working together on mortgage issues, an effort coordinated within a mere two week span. With explicit constitutional authority to coordinate the enforcement of uniform state laws and regulations, there is no reason a distant and self interested federal government can't be relieved of these duties and permitted to focus its efforts on matters of national importance. This proposal anticipates the transfer of federal facilities housing the various bureaucratic functions to the states as well.

By the amendment, all federal statutes and their regulations enacted under the interstate commerce clause she be deemed adopted by the various states. This shall provide continuity and coordination of administration of these laws until they such time as the states decide to abandon or modify such laws. Certainly reasonable men can agree on rules to effectuate the transfer, and for the subsequent co-ordination of tax receipt planning by the States and the Federal governments.

WE DEMAND ACCESS AND ACCOUNTABILITY

The next question will be "But will this make a difference if the same laws and regulations are in effect, only that they are now enforced by coordinated state law instead of federal law?" It's a valid point to raise, but the first answer is by a question in response, and that is "How can it not be better in overall and cumulative effect?" The county is on the wrong path. Most of the states are required by their own constitutions to balance their budgets, and while they have figured out how to take on debt anyway, they do have more recent experience balancing their budgets than the federal government does. In addition, over time, they will be more responsive to taxpayers probing the reason for tax revenues that can't be justified. There is a whole senate at the state level, and that means that there is a state senator's office within a short drive of where I live or where you live. There are even more representatives at the statehouse, and if I don't know one personally, probably my neighbor does. Yes, some states are ill-governed. But many are not ill governed, and to relieve the states of mandates, and to let the well governed states flourish, will set a standard and guide for the other states to achieve also.

OTHER CONSIDERATIONS

Consideration should be given to a new branch of government, a banking and finance branch, in recognition of both the critical functions that money and capital perform in our society, and the need to isolate the management of those functions from the risk of political tampering and miscalculation, the inclination to which has been bred into our politicians. Discipline in our financial affairs, so starkly missing in the current circumstances, is required if our country is again going to grow and provide a bright and prosperous future for our children. The ability to manipulate our economy for short term political gain will become that much more enticing a tool for the politicians to use when facing the prospect with a large swath of governmental funding being transferred to the states. By forming a new branch of government, not only will the banking and financial functions be protected from these attempts, it will give cover to those in government who do not wish to disrupt our national banking system but are being pressured by constituents and other special interest groups. Since the only long term benefit that the banking and financial sectors can provide to the nation is derived from providing a well managed and sound currency, and the provision of safeguards and appropriate oversight of reserves, the banking and financial branch's mission shall be limited to those functions. The allocation of credit is in all normal circumstances a cynical misnomer, as it is actually the misallocation of credit, and therefore beyond the purpose of government. In the case of a presidential declaration of necessity a broader scope of authority can be permitted until the exigent circumstances abate. For the rest of the time trust in the people and their industry and motivation is the surest way to prosperity, faster and with greater and more lasting effects than the governmental manipulations now utilized at times of crisis to squander our resources and reward those loyal and beholden to a political party. The scope of authority of this new branch of government shall extend to the safekeeping of deposits and to all those pools of funds involving the public and used in a manner that result in the creation of credit.

Having misallocated credit so badly by sabotaging good banking practices in the housing industry, the government wishes to take this expertise and put it to good use allocating consumer credit through the new Consumer Financial Protection Bureau. Whether this is sound policy or not, the person given such broad power has not been subject to the constitutionally required confirmation by the Senate. By merely avoiding the title of "Director" the thought is that this voids the role of the Senate under the Constitution Article II, Section 2. A determination by the Supreme Court as to whether a Senate confirmation vote is required can clear up the authority of this "Presidential Assistant" so that clarity exists as to the validity of regulations and administrative rulings. It would be best that the structures and procedures in the Constitution were held to be applicable in the face of such a transparent ruse. The Constitution is the bulwark that protects us against the human tendency to usurp power, but it only works when the Courts have the courage to confront the executive branch on behalf of the people.

Consideration should be given to facilitate and ease the passage of federal funding legislation. Such facilitation will help maintain in a strong manner the federal functions that do remain, including the military and intelligence functions. This redirection of federal attention to essential matters and the clear funding provided by the states to the federal government to carry out those functions should start to shore up our ability to meet the external challenges of the future.

Recess appointments should be abolished. So called "recess appointments", used to by-pass debate in congress for Presidential appointments serve no good function. Long gone are the days Congress would not be in session for lengthy periods due to the time to travel by horseback.

Likewise, the people need to confirm that the government does not have the power to do that which is "necessary and proper" as a separate and discretionary grant of power as our government would like, but rather it stands only to implement other powers granted in the Constitution.

Maintenance of the social security system shall remain in the federal government with funding provided by the states to the federal government for a period of twenty four years after enactment of this amendment, and thereafter its maintenance shall be transferred to the individual states acting initially in consort, with normal retirement adjusted annually to an agreed upon percentage of the normal life expectancy.

So that environment laws may not be used by the federal government as a means to regulate and tax, since virtually all human activity, even sleep, effects the environment, we call for jurisdiction of all environmental matters shall be with the States. While we all want the cleanest, most pristine and healthful environment possible, the wisdom of the judicious policy of balancing of environmental and economic concerns provided in the National Environmental Policy Act of 1969, and which has provided us with a robust economy such as to financially support environmental efforts, has all be been abandoned. In its place we see proposed regulations that have the ability to devastate entire industries, placing more out of work and further exacerbating our enormous debt while reducing our resources available to support environmental concerns. Conflicts between the States resulting from environmental actions can be resolved in a federal environmental court having original and exclusive jurisdiction under Article 3 of the Constitution.

The explicit authority for the States, by agreement, to combine and coordinate regulatory functions as to the matters before them should be confirmed.

Substantially greater penalties, including stiff jail terms, need to be enacted for the types of intentional, systematic and substantial vote fraud now taking place. It's clear that vote fraud has become a serious matter within the United States, even to the extent that it has affected the functioning of the Senate skewing the results of filibuster attempts. This democracy will not survive if contempt for the integrity of the voting process is only cosmetically challenged or actively supported, especially if by the Justice Department. Maybe it is no coincidence that attempts to disenfranchise the voters on such scale are occurring at the same time as the government exhibits such distain for dialogue, disagreement and the dissemination of opinions critical to itself and its policies. Obstruction of process and the hindrance of the flow of information to the public -other than that information understandably controlled for national security purposes - contribute to and enhance the vortex of mistrust that will destroy the good and effective functioning of government.

Consideration should be given to repeal of the 17th Amendment, which provided for the direct election of Senators. As originally structured the state legislators chose the senators and the people elected the members of the House of Representatives. Taking that power away from the states served to further emasculate the states in their dealings with the federal government, removing a valuable counterweight in our system of checks and balances.

BEYOND THE MONEY

The political culture has declined to the point where the object is no longer to serve the will and attend to the needs of the people, but rather to serve the will and attend to the needs of those who are in office. So the ballot counts are contaminated by voter fraud, both of the false or ineligible voter brand and of the military uniform and night-stick kind. But beyond that attempts to coercive union membership by "check-card" so as to eliminate secret ballots, boycotts of companies for political purposes, regulatory threats, attempts to misuse the IRS against opponents, suppression of speech by regulators and politicians, attempts to legislate against free political speech, threats, patently baseless claims of criminal violations......

This is the post-partisan world the people were promised? What are they doing to America? Where is the basic decency?

WE DEMAND A GOVERNMENT THAT WORKS

The American people need a return to a functioning government, one where policy debates are principled, and when the debate concludes there is some capacity to agree upon what appears to be in the interest of the nation - beyond and above the interests of the political parties or the individual politicians involved. The proposal envisions the federal government portfolio of responsibilities to include matters within the skies and heavens, matters from our shores and borders outward, communications and postal functions, homeland security functions, monetary and financial stability functions, cyber-warfare preparedness, the federal judiciary, and patent issuances and intellectual property rights registrations. The list is limited to those elements essential to the nation that can only be performed only by a central government and none other, so as to bring focus and execution to achievement of our national needs and purposes. Included in this list will be the power to raise armies (the draft if necessary), take the census count, and to provide specifications for state issued identification cards, usually driver's license cards, for homeland security purposes. The balance of functions shall be reserved to the states and to individuals.

WE OWE A LOT OF MONEY NOW

The sovereign debt of the United States shall continue to be issued by and in the name of the federal government, and such claim shall be repayable to the federal government by a claim against the state treasuries in proportion to their populations, unless the states otherwise agree upon a different method of allocation. The ceiling for debt and for the accumulated non-debt obligations of the federal government shall not be increased without being initiated by the states and passed by three fifths of the states. The States and the Federal government will need to coordinate their budgetary requirements.

There is **nothing** in any of these proposals, either the actual transfer of functions or the in the functioning of governmental dealings thereafter, that cannot be accomplished by men whose efforts are dedicated to the citizens of this nation.

YES, RIGHT NOW, THIS MOMENT

If you could time travel, and return to this country in fifty years, seeing your children grown up and dealing with the burdens of raising families themselves and trying to provide your grandchildren or great-grandchildren with a better future, what would you see? In a larger sense you would see three hundred and fifty millions Americans, maybe more, who would be going about their jobs in a society organized under certain principles. And hopefully those principles will provide for freedoms and liberties, prosperity, and a secure future. If that future is going to be a bright future, when are we going to repair the manner in which our country is functioning? Is there any benefit to delay beyond this very moment to make the requisite changes?

It is now time to de-federalize our country. What do we have to lose, daring to change? The only thing we will lose is the sure collapse of this great country's potential and the failure of the American Dream if we stay on our present course. Watch the fear and confusion as you take your money back, they will be filling sandbags of empty logic eighteen hours a day, or twenty four hours per day if you wish to take into account the all night news clips. They will bring up a myriad of detailed activities that will be nettlesome to transfer. They want you to be afraid. But there is no need to be afraid since well intentioned and motivated men and women will find the necessary ways and means to serve the nation's needs. It is time to complete Ronald Reagan's vision of respect for the 10th Amendment. Is any state afraid to stand up to the tyrant within? Is there fear of federal retribution? The people are confident in taking care of themselves. They are confident that a vibrant society can again be ours. The people are confident that by taking care of themselves they can once again feel prosperity, and can take care of the poor more effectively than has been done by a distant government, this confidence resulting from the bounty of the nation and the charitable character of our people. It is time to get passed the period of national outrage, to take control of our circumstances, and to get back to reasoned consideration of matters of high national importance.

People are now taking up this cause. It can be seen in New Jersey and Nevada and Alaska and Minnesota and Kentucky and Virginia and in many other places, and in the fervent hearts and faces of those you see on your newscasts, who know this is, indeed, the time.

IT IS OUR RESPONSIBILITY, WE THE PEOPLE

It is up to us, the people, to take responsibility at this point. There are no other solutions. Letting the government rummage around in the vault of the national wealth and then expecting them to be disciplined about using your money when it's in their hands is asking the impossible You can't take aspirin for cancer, nor can you take out eighty percent of a cancerous tumor and leave the rest. It is up to us the people. We are the radical center. Now is the time. Now is the time *to act!* The constitution is the law of the people, the law that the people have imposed upon their government. The government is now intoxicated with vast sums of money, to the point of impoverishing the nation by drawing excess resources beyond that which are needed for proper governance. The government is showing disregard for the will of the people and the Constitutional law imposed upon that government by the people. The people are now going to demonstrate their power over those who distain the role and the privilege of government service bestowed upon them. The American people will not suffer fools or failure, and will not tolerate an insulated and messianic government.

WE ARE IN CONTROL, NOT THE POLITICIANS

It is now time for the people to recognize that we are both subject to the law of the land, and when we speak together, we also create, control and amend that law, and it is to serve us. The people chose their representatives at the various states, and they in turn met to create the Constitution.

....

We *created* the Constitution:

THE PEOPLE

⇓

States

⇓

Constitution

The Constitution is the Supreme Law of the land, other laws may not conflict with the Constitution, and all, *including the government*, must obey the Constitution and laws of the land.

<u>We *obey* the Constitution</u>:

THE CONSTITUTION

⇩

Laws

⇩

People and Government

<u>We *AMEND* the Constitution</u>:

THE PEOPLE

States or Congress

Constitution

The Constitution structures all the governmental components of the nation, and, *along with those governmental components*, **it serves the people**.

WE ARE THE PEOPLE

The Federal Government and our constitution exist to serve the peoples of this nation. It is the creation of the people of the United States, and it is ours to change as needed. This is one of those times that cry out for repair of our nation by repair of our highest law and modification of the conduct of those who serve in government under that law. There is much that is right with America, and chief among them are our values and character. We have been blessed with many advantages found nowhere else on the earth in the same combination, and across the world despite the scurrilous comments of petty dictators and the speeches of national leaders grandstanding for some segment of their electorate, the world needs the United States to lead as it always has, with principle, with selflessness, purposeful and resolute in our will to bring about justice. Absent American leadership, there are risks now existent such as the world has not seen.

In the introduction to "Common Sense", Thomas Paine says "In this first parliament, every man by natural right has a seat". He refers to the authority of government emanating from the people, and that that authority ultimately stays with the people. We do need laws and we do need government, but we retain the right to modify and fix that government so that it serves the needs of the people. We do not need utopian saviors and we don't need mandates and orders from those we elect to power. The grandest Utopian vision the earth has seen until this time was that of the Soviet Union. The United States does not need a vision of change to be engineered by a government self-inflated in its own image. The United States needs the energy and courage of its people.

"If there must be trouble, let it be in my day, that my child may have peace."

Thomas Paine, The American Crisis, No. 1, December 19, 1776

It is now up to us, and up to the state governments, so emasculated and drained up to this point, to propose and pass amendments to our constitution as the people ultimately demand. There is a groundswell in the country, rumblings that hint at the discontent of the people and the demand for a return to them of their country. There is no reason whatsoever that these three hundred million people cannot adopt a sensible course for our common future, apply our energies to our common future, and become stronger for having gone through this distortion in our national life. This country remains for now the beacon of hope and the shining example of the possibilities of freedom and achievement in the world, still the dream of many across the globe, where all are accepted, and where government is to serve the people instead of the other way around. We owe to ourselves this change we embark upon, we owe it to our future, we owe it out of our sense of responsibility, and we owe it to our children. There can be no waffling on our responsibilities. The course will be very hard. And that is exactly why we can accomplish this task. We can do it exactly because it is momentous, and because we are Americans, and because that's what Americans do. We are the nation of Pat Tillman, who gave up a lucrative NFL career to serve his country and ended up killed in Afghanistan. We are the nation of Todd Beamer who sacrificed his life overwhelming the terrorists controlling flight 93 over Pennsylvania, starting with his acclimation "Let's Roll!" and the actions that followed wrestling control of the falling aircraft. We are the nation of Tom Little, an American optometrist working in Afghanistan to help the people there in spite of the obvious danger, who lost his life there this summer of 2010. We are the nation of Salvatore Giunta who is receiving the Medal of Honor for courage and leadership under extreme enemy fire. We need to honor these men, and we need to act for our whole nation, for ourselves, and to relieve our leaders of the temptations of self interest and other conflicts of interest in which they are placed, and to restore clarity of thought and risk assessment. Time stares at us as the projected numbers of our future, while on the current path, threaten a collision that will remove the control of our destiny that America has always enjoyed. We now have the opportunity, the energy, and the desire to right that which is wrong, and which has been wrong for so long. Looking back for purposes of finding fault or responsibility for bringing us to the state we are in would be a distraction and a deflection of energy and purpose. Our sight must be kept looking forward to our future. Our concern is to correct our path, while we can. There are those who might argue as to some of the details stated, but the error of our current path is undeniable, and the feasibility of the solution is clear to all but those who do not wish a solution, or who desire those solutions whose lack of effectiveness has been proven.

"The cause of America is in a great measure the cause of all mankind."

Thomas Paine, Common Sense, 1776

The Constitution of the United States:

A Transcription

Note: *The following text is a transcription of the Constitution in its original form.*
NOTE → *Items that are underlined have since been amended or superseded.*

We the People of the United States, in Order to form a more perfect Union, establish Justice, insure domestic Tranquility, provide for the common defence, promote the general Welfare, and secure the Blessings of Liberty to ourselves and our Posterity, do ordain and establish this Constitution for the United States of America.

Article. I.

Section. 1.

All legislative Powers herein granted shall be vested in a Congress of the United States, which shall consist of a Senate and House of Representatives.

Section. 2.

The House of Representatives shall be composed of Members chosen every second Year by the People of the several States, and the Electors in each State shall have the Qualifications requisite for Electors of the most numerous Branch of the State Legislature.

No Person shall be a Representative who shall not have attained to the Age of twenty five Years, and been seven Years a Citizen of the United States, and who shall not, when elected, be an Inhabitant of that State in which he shall be chosen.

Representatives and direct Taxes shall be apportioned among the several States which may be included within this Union, according to their respective Numbers, which shall be determined by adding to the whole Number of free Persons, including those bound to Service for a Term of Years, and excluding Indians not taxed, three fifths of all other Persons. The actual Enumeration shall be made within three Years after the first Meeting of the Congress of the United States, and within every subsequent Term of ten Years, in such Manner as they shall by Law direct. The Number of Representatives shall not exceed one for every thirty Thousand, but each State shall have at Least one Representative; and until such enumeration shall be made, the State of New Hampshire shall be entitled to chuse three, Massachusetts eight, Rhode-Island and Providence Plantations one, Connecticut five, New-York six, New Jersey four, Pennsylvania eight, Delaware one, Maryland six, Virginia ten, North Carolina five, South Carolina five, and Georgia three.

When vacancies happen in the Representation from any State, the Executive Authority thereof shall issue Writs of Election to fill such Vacancies.

The House of Representatives shall choose their Speaker and other Officers; and shall have the sole Power of Impeachment.

Section. 3.

The Senate of the United States shall be composed of two Senators from each State, chosen by the Legislature thereof for six Years; and each Senator shall have one Vote.

Immediately after they shall be assembled in Consequence of the first Election, they shall be divided as equally as may be into three Classes. The Seats of the Senators of the first Class shall be vacated at the Expiration of the second Year, of the second Class at the Expiration of the fourth Year, and of the third Class at the Expiration of the sixth Year, so that one third may be chosen every second Year; and if Vacancies happen by Resignation, or otherwise, during the Recess of the Legislature of any State, the Executive thereof may make temporary Appointments until the next Meeting of the Legislature, which shall then fill such Vacancies.

No Person shall be a Senator who shall not have attained to the Age of thirty Years, and been nine Years a Citizen of the United States, and who shall not, when elected, be an Inhabitant of that State for which he shall be chosen.

The Vice President of the United States shall be President of the Senate, but shall have no Vote, unless they be equally divided.

The Senate shall chuse their other Officers, and also a President pro tempore, in the Absence of the Vice President, or when he shall exercise the Office of President of the United States.

The Senate shall have the sole Power to try all Impeachments. When sitting for that Purpose, they shall be on Oath or Affirmation. When the President of the United States is tried, the Chief Justice shall preside: And no Person shall be convicted without the Concurrence of two thirds of the Members present.

Judgment in Cases of Impeachment shall not extend further than to removal from Office, and disqualification to hold and enjoy any Office of honor, Trust or Profit under the United States: but the Party convicted shall nevertheless be liable and subject to Indictment, Trial, Judgment and Punishment, according to Law.

Section. 4.

The Times, Places and Manner of holding Elections for Senators and Representatives, shall be prescribed in each State by the Legislature thereof; but the Congress may at any time by Law make or alter such Regulations, except as to the Places of choosing Senators.

The Congress shall assemble at least once in every Year, and such Meeting shall be on the first Monday in December, unless they shall by Law appoint a different Day.

Section. 5.

Each House shall be the Judge of the Elections, Returns and Qualifications of its own Members, and a Majority of each shall constitute a Quorum to do Business; but a smaller Number may adjourn from day to day, and may be authorized to compel the Attendance of absent Members, in such Manner, and under such Penalties as each House may provide.

Each House may determine the Rules of its Proceedings, punish its Members for disorderly Behaviour, and, with the Concurrence of two thirds, expel a Member.

Each House shall keep a Journal of its Proceedings, and from time to time publish the same, excepting such Parts as may in their Judgment require Secrecy; and the Yeas and Nays of the Members of either House on any question shall, at the Desire of one fifth of those Present, be entered on the Journal.

Neither House, during the Session of Congress, shall, without the Consent of the other, adjourn for more than three days, nor to any other Place than that in which the two Houses shall be sitting.

Section. 6.

The Senators and Representatives shall receive a Compensation for their Services, to be ascertained by Law, and paid out of the Treasury of the United States. They shall in all Cases, except Treason, Felony and Breach of the Peace, be privileged from Arrest during their Attendance at the Session of their respective Houses, and in going to and returning from the same; and for any Speech or Debate in either House, they shall not be questioned in any other Place.

No Senator or Representative shall, during the Time for which he was elected, be appointed to any civil Office under the Authority of the United States, which shall have been created, or the Emoluments whereof shall have been increased during such time; and no Person holding any Office under the United States, shall be a Member of either House during his Continuance in Office.

Section. 7.

All Bills for raising Revenue shall originate in the House of Representatives; but the Senate may propose or concur with Amendments as on other Bills.

Every Bill which shall have passed the House of Representatives and the Senate, shall, before it become a Law, be presented to the President of the United States: If he approve he shall sign it, but if not he shall return it, with his Objections to that House in which it shall have originated, who shall enter the Objections at large on their Journal, and proceed to reconsider it. If after such Reconsideration two thirds of that House shall agree to pass the Bill, it shall be sent, together with the Objections, to the other House, by which it shall likewise be reconsidered, and if approved by two thirds of that House, it shall become a Law. But in all such Cases the Votes of both Houses shall be determined by yeas and Nays, and the Names of the Persons voting for and against the Bill shall be entered on the Journal of each House respectively. If any Bill shall not be returned by the President within ten Days (Sundays excepted) after it shall have been presented to him, the Same shall be a Law, in like Manner as if he had signed it, unless the Congress by their Adjournment prevent its Return, in which Case it shall not be a Law.

Every Order, Resolution, or Vote to which the Concurrence of the Senate and House of Representatives may be necessary (except on a question of Adjournment) shall be presented to the President of the United States; and before the Same shall take Effect, shall be approved by him, or being disapproved by him, shall be repassed by two thirds of the Senate and House of Representatives, according to the Rules and Limitations prescribed in the Case of a Bill.

Section. 8.

The Congress shall have Power To lay and collect Taxes, Duties, Imposts and Excises, to pay the Debts and provide for the common Defence and general Welfare of the United States; but all Duties, Imposts and Excises shall be uniform throughout the United States;

To borrow Money on the credit of the United States;

To regulate Commerce with foreign Nations, and among the several States, and with the Indian Tribes;

To establish an uniform Rule of Naturalization, and uniform Laws on the subject of Bankruptcies throughout the United States;

To coin Money, regulate the Value thereof, and of foreign Coin, and fix the Standard of Weights and Measures;

To provide for the Punishment of counterfeiting the Securities and current Coin of the United States;

To establish Post Offices and post Roads;

To promote the Progress of Science and useful Arts, by securing for limited Times to Authors and Inventors the exclusive Right to their respective Writings and Discoveries;

To constitute Tribunals inferior to the supreme Court;

To define and punish Piracies and Felonies committed on the high Seas, and Offences against the Law of Nations;

To declare War, grant Letters of Marque and Reprisal, and make Rules concerning Captures on Land and Water;

To raise and support Armies, but no Appropriation of Money to that Use shall be for a longer Term than two Years;

To provide and maintain a Navy;

To make Rules for the Government and Regulation of the land and naval Forces;

To provide for calling forth the Militia to execute the Laws of the Union, suppress Insurrections and repel Invasions;

To provide for organizing, arming, and disciplining, the Militia, and for governing such Part of them as may be employed in the Service of the United States, reserving to the States respectively, the Appointment of the Officers, and the Authority of training the Militia according to the discipline prescribed by Congress;

To exercise exclusive Legislation in all Cases whatsoever, over such District (not exceeding ten Miles square) as may, by Cession of particular States, and the Acceptance of Congress, become the Seat of the Government of the United States, and to exercise like Authority over all Places purchased by the Consent of the Legislature of the State in which the Same shall be, for the Erection of Forts, Magazines, Arsenals, dock-Yards, and other needful Buildings;--And

To make all Laws which shall be necessary and proper for carrying into Execution the foregoing Powers, and all other Powers vested by this Constitution in the Government of the United States, or in any Department or Officer thereof.

Section. 9.

The Migration or Importation of such Persons as any of the States now existing shall think proper to admit, shall not be prohibited by the Congress prior to the Year one thousand eight hundred and eight, but a Tax or duty may be imposed on such Importation, not exceeding ten dollars for each Person.

The Privilege of the Writ of Habeas Corpus shall not be suspended, unless when in Cases of Rebellion or Invasion the public Safety may require it.

No Bill of Attainder or ex post facto Law shall be passed.

No Capitation, or other direct, Tax shall be laid, unless in Proportion to the Census or enumeration herein before directed to be taken.

No Tax or Duty shall be laid on Articles exported from any State.

No Preference shall be given by any Regulation of Commerce or Revenue to the Ports of one State over those of another; nor shall

Vessels bound to, or from, one State, be obliged to enter, clear, or pay Duties in another.

No Money shall be drawn from the Treasury, but in Consequence of Appropriations made by Law; and a regular Statement and Account of the Receipts and Expenditures of all public Money shall be published from time to time.

No Title of Nobility shall be granted by the United States: And no Person holding any Office of Profit or Trust under them, shall, without the Consent of the Congress, accept of any present, Emolument, Office, or Title, of any kind whatever, from any King, Prince, or foreign State.

Section. 10.

No State shall enter into any Treaty, Alliance, or Confederation; grant Letters of Marque and Reprisal; coin Money; emit Bills of Credit; make any Thing but gold and silver Coin a Tender in Payment of Debts; pass any Bill of Attainder, ex post facto Law, or Law impairing the Obligation of Contracts, or grant any Title of Nobility.

No State shall, without the Consent of the Congress, lay any Imposts or Duties on Imports or Exports, except what may be absolutely necessary for executing it's inspection Laws: and the net Produce of all Duties and Imposts, laid by any State on Imports or Exports, shall be for the Use of the Treasury of the United States; and all such Laws shall be subject to the Revision and Control of the Congress.

No State shall, without the Consent of Congress, lay any Duty of Tonnage, keep Troops, or Ships of War in time of Peace, enter into any Agreement or Compact with another State, or with a foreign Power, or engage in War, unless actually invaded, or in such imminent Danger as will not admit of delay.

Article. II.

Section. 1.

The executive Power shall be vested in a President of the United States of America. He shall hold his Office during the Term of four Years, and, together with the Vice President, chosen for the same Term, be elected, as follows:

Each State shall appoint, in such Manner as the Legislature thereof may direct, a Number of Electors, equal to the whole Number of Senators and Representatives to which the State may be entitled in the Congress: but no Senator or Representative, or Person holding an Office of Trust or Profit under the United States, shall be appointed an Elector.

The Electors shall meet in their respective States, and vote by Ballot for two Persons, of whom one at least shall not be an Inhabitant of the same State with themselves. And they shall make a List of all the Persons voted for, and of the Number of Votes for each; which List they shall sign and certify, and transmit sealed to the Seat of the Government of the United States, directed to the President of the Senate. The President of the Senate shall, in the Presence of the Senate and House of Representatives, open all the Certificates, and the Votes shall then be counted. The Person having the greatest Number of Votes shall be the President, if such Number be a Majority of the whole Number of Electors appointed; and if there be more than one who have such Majority, and have an equal Number of Votes, then the House of Representatives shall immediately chuse by Ballot one of them for President; and if no Person have a Majority, then from the five highest on the List the said House shall in like Manner chuse the President. But in chusing the President, the Votes shall be taken by States, the Representation from each State having one Vote; A quorum for this purpose shall consist of a Member or Members from two thirds of the States, and a Majority of all the States shall be necessary to a Choice. In every Case, after the Choice of the President, the Person having the greatest Number of Votes of the Electors shall be the Vice President.

But if there should remain two or more who have equal Votes, the Senate shall choose from them by Ballot the Vice President.

The Congress may determine the Time of chusing the Electors, and the Day on which they shall give their Votes; which Day shall be the same throughout the United States.

No Person except a natural born Citizen, or a Citizen of the United States, at the time of the Adoption of this Constitution, shall be eligible to the Office of President; neither shall any Person be eligible to that Office who shall not have attained to the Age of thirty five Years, and been fourteen Years a Resident within the United States.

In Case of the Removal of the President from Office, or of his Death, Resignation, or Inability to discharge the Powers and Duties of the said Office, the Same shall devolve on the Vice President, and the Congress may by Law provide for the Case of Removal, Death, Resignation or Inability, both of the President and Vice President, declaring what Officer shall then act as President, and such Officer shall act accordingly, until the Disability be removed, or a President shall be elected.

The President shall, at stated Times, receive for his Services, a Compensation, which shall neither be increased nor diminished during the Period for which he shall have been elected, and he shall not receive within that Period any other Emolument from the United States, or any of them.

Before he enter on the Execution of his Office, he shall take the following Oath or Affirmation:--"I do solemnly swear (or affirm) that I will faithfully execute the Office of President of the United States, and will to the best of my Ability, preserve, protect and defend the Constitution of the United States."

Section. 2.

The President shall be Commander in Chief of the Army and Navy of the United States, and of the Militia of the several States, when called into the actual Service of the United States; he may require the Opinion, in writing, of the principal Officer in each of the executive Departments, upon any Subject relating to the Duties of their respective Offices, and he shall have Power to grant Reprieves and Pardons for Offences against the United States, except in Cases of Impeachment.

He shall have Power, by and with the Advice and Consent of the Senate, to make Treaties, provided two thirds of the Senators present concur; and he shall nominate, and by and with the Advice and Consent of the Senate, shall appoint Ambassadors, other public Ministers and Consuls, Judges of the supreme Court, and all other Officers of the United States, whose Appointments are not herein otherwise provided for, and which shall be established by Law: but the Congress may by Law vest the Appointment of such inferior Officers, as they think proper, in the President alone, in the Courts of Law, or in the Heads of Departments.

The President shall have Power to fill up all Vacancies that may happen during the Recess of the Senate, by granting Commissions which shall expire at the End of their next Session.

Section. 3.

He shall from time to time give to the Congress Information of the State of the Union, and recommend to their Consideration such Measures as he shall judge necessary and expedient; he may, on extraordinary Occasions, convene both Houses, or either of them, and in Case of Disagreement between them, with Respect to the Time of Adjournment, he may adjourn them to such Time as he shall think proper; he shall receive Ambassadors and other public Ministers; he shall take Care that the Laws be faithfully executed, and shall Commission all the Officers of the United States.

Section. 4.

The President, Vice President and all civil Officers of the United States, shall be removed from Office on Impeachment for, and Conviction of, Treason, Bribery, or other high Crimes and Misdemeanors.

Article III.

Section. 1.

The judicial Power of the United States shall be vested in one supreme Court, and in such inferior Courts as the Congress may from time to time ordain and establish. The Judges, both of the supreme and inferior Courts, shall hold their Offices during good Behavior, and shall, at stated Times, receive for their Services a Compensation, which shall not be diminished during their Continuance in Office.

Section. 2.

The judicial Power shall extend to all Cases, in Law and Equity, arising under this Constitution, the Laws of the United States, and Treaties made, or which shall be made, under their Authority;--to all Cases affecting Ambassadors, other public Ministers and Consuls;--to all Cases of admiralty and maritime Jurisdiction;--to Controversies to which the United States shall be a Party;--to Controversies between two or more States;-- between a State and Citizens of another State,--between Citizens of different States,--between Citizens of the same State claiming Lands under Grants of different States, and between a State, or the Citizens thereof, and foreign States, Citizens or Subjects.

In all Cases affecting Ambassadors, other public Ministers and Consuls, and those in which a State shall be Party, the supreme Court shall have original Jurisdiction. In all the other Cases before mentioned, the Supreme Court shall have appellate Jurisdiction, both as to Law and Fact, with such Exceptions, and under such Regulations as the Congress shall make.

The Trial of all Crimes, except in Cases of Impeachment, shall be by Jury; and such Trial shall be held in the State where the said Crimes shall have been committed; but when not committed within any State, the Trial shall be at such Place or Places as the Congress may by Law have directed.

Section. 3.

Treason against the United States, shall consist only in levying War against them, or in adhering to their Enemies, giving them Aid and Comfort. No Person shall be convicted of Treason unless on the Testimony of two Witnesses to the same overt Act, or on Confession in open Court.

The Congress shall have Power to declare the Punishment of Treason, but no Attainder of Treason shall work Corruption of Blood, or Forfeiture except during the Life of the Person attainted.

Article. IV.

Section. 1.

Full Faith and Credit shall be given in each State to the public Acts, Records, and judicial Proceedings of every other State. And the Congress may by general Laws prescribe the Manner in which such Acts, Records and Proceedings shall be proved, and the Effect thereof.

Section. 2.

The Citizens of each State shall be entitled to all Privileges and Immunities of Citizens in the several States.

A Person charged in any State with Treason, Felony, or other Crime, who shall flee from Justice, and be found in another State, shall on Demand of the executive Authority of the State from which he fled, be delivered up, to be removed to the State having Jurisdiction of the Crime.

No Person held to Service or Labour in one State, under the Laws thereof, escaping into another, shall, in Consequence of any Law or Regulation therein, be discharged from such Service or Labour, but shall be delivered up on Claim of the Party to whom such Service or Labour may be due.

Section. 3.

New States may be admitted by the Congress into this Union; but no new State shall be formed or erected within the Jurisdiction of any other State; nor any State be formed by the Junction of two or more States, or Parts of States, without the Consent of the Legislatures of the States concerned as well as of the Congress.

The Congress shall have Power to dispose of and make all needful Rules and Regulations respecting the Territory or other Property belonging to the United States; and nothing in this Constitution shall be so construed as to Prejudice any Claims of the United States, or of any particular State.

Section. 4.

The United States shall guarantee to every State in this Union a Republican Form of Government, and shall protect each of them against Invasion; and on Application of the Legislature, or of the Executive (when the Legislature cannot be convened), against domestic Violence.

Article. V.

The Congress, whenever two thirds of both Houses shall deem it necessary, shall propose Amendments to this Constitution, or, on the Application of the Legislatures of two thirds of the several States, shall call a Convention for proposing Amendments, which, in either Case, shall be valid to all Intents and Purposes, as Part of this Constitution, when ratified by the Legislatures of three fourths of the several States, or by Conventions in three fourths thereof, as the one or the other Mode of Ratification may be proposed by the Congress; Provided that no Amendment which may be made prior to the Year One thousand eight hundred and eight shall in any Manner affect the first and fourth Clauses in the Ninth Section of the first Article; and that no State, without its Consent, shall be deprived of its equal Suffrage in the Senate.

Article. VI.

All Debts contracted and Engagements entered into, before the Adoption of this Constitution, shall be as valid against the United States under this Constitution, as under the Confederation.

This Constitution, and the Laws of the United States which shall be made in Pursuance thereof; and all Treaties made, or which shall be made, under the Authority of the United States, shall be the supreme Law of the Land; and the Judges in every State shall be bound thereby, any Thing in the Constitution or Laws of any State to the Contrary notwithstanding.

The Senators and Representatives before mentioned, and the Members of the several State Legislatures, and all executive and judicial Officers, both of the United States and of the several States, shall be bound by Oath or Affirmation, to support this Constitution; but no religious Test shall ever be required as a Qualification to any Office or public Trust under the United States.

Article. VII.

The Ratification of the Conventions of nine States, shall be sufficient for the Establishment of this Constitution between the States so ratifying the Same.

The Word, "the," being interlined between the seventh and eighth Lines of the first Page, the Word "Thirty" being partly written on an Erasure in the fifteenth Line of the first Page, The Words "is tried" being interlined between the thirty second and thirty third Lines of the first Page and the Word "the" being interlined between the forty third and forty fourth Lines of the second Page.

Attest William Jackson Secretary

done in Convention by the Unanimous Consent of the States present the Seventeenth Day of September in the Year of our Lord one thousand seven hundred and Eighty seven and of the Independence of the United States of America the Twelfth In witness whereof We have hereunto subscribed our Names,

G°. Washington
Presidt and deputy from Virginia

Delaware
Geo: Read
Gunning Bedford jun
John Dickinson
Richard Bassett
Jaco: Broom

Maryland
James McHenry
Dan of St Thos. Jenifer
Danl. Carroll

Virginia
John Blair
James Madison Jr.

North Carolina
Wm. Blount
Richd. Dobbs Spaight
Hu Williamson

South Carolina
J. Rutledge
Charles Cotesworth Pinckney
Charles Pinckney
Pierce Butler

Georgia
William Few
Abr Baldwin

New Hampshire
John Langdon
Nicholas Gilman

Massachusetts
Nathaniel Gorham
Rufus King

Connecticut
Wm. Saml. Johnson
Roger Sherman

New York
Alexander Hamilton

New Jersey
Wil: Livingston
David Brearley
Wm. Paterson
Jona: Dayton

Pennsylvania
B Franklin
Thomas Mifflin
Robt. Morris
Geo. Clymer
Thos. FitzSimons
Jared Ingersoll
James Wilson
Gouv Morris

The Bill of Rights: A Transcription

The Preamble to The Bill of Rights

Congress   of   the   **United**   **States** begun and held at the City of New-York, on Wednesday the fourth of March, one thousand seven hundred and eighty nine.

THE Conventions of a number of the States, having at the time of their adopting the Constitution, expressed a desire, in order to prevent misconstruction or abuse of its powers, that further declaratory and restrictive clauses should be added: And as extending the ground of public confidence in the Government, will best ensure the beneficent ends of its institution.

RESOLVED by the Senate and House of Representatives of the United States of America, in Congress assembled, two thirds of both Houses concurring, that the following Articles be proposed to the Legislatures of the several States, as amendments to the Constitution of the United States, all, or any of which Articles, when ratified by three fourths of the said Legislatures, to be valid to all intents and purposes, as part of the said Constitution; viz.

ARTICLES in addition to, and Amendment of the Constitution of the United States of America, proposed by Congress, and ratified by the Legislatures of the several States, pursuant to the fifth Article of the original Constitution.

Note: The following text is a transcription of the first ten amendments to the Constitution in their original form. These amendments were ratified December 15, 1791, and form what is known as the "Bill of Rights."

Amendment I

Congress shall make no law respecting an establishment of religion, or prohibiting the free exercise thereof; or abridging the freedom of speech, or of the press; or the right of the people peaceably to assemble, and to petition the Government for a redress of grievances.

Amendment II

A well regulated Militia, being necessary to the security of a free State, the right of the people to keep and bear Arms, shall not be infringed.

Amendment III

No Soldier shall, in time of peace be quartered in any house, without the consent of the Owner, nor in time of war, but in a manner to be prescribed by law.

Amendment IV

The right of the people to be secure in their persons, houses, papers, and effects, against unreasonable searches and seizures, shall not be violated, and no Warrants shall issue, but upon probable cause, supported by Oath or affirmation, and particularly describing the place to be searched, and the persons or things to be seized.

Amendment V

No person shall be held to answer for a capital, or otherwise infamous crime, unless on a presentment or indictment of a Grand Jury, except in cases arising in the land or naval forces, or in the Militia, when in actual service in time of War or public danger; nor shall any person be subject for the same offence to be twice put in jeopardy of life or limb; nor shall be compelled in any criminal case to be a witness against himself, nor be deprived of life, liberty, or property, without due process of law; nor shall private property be taken for public use, without just compensation.

Amendment VI

In all criminal prosecutions, the accused shall enjoy the right to a speedy and public trial, by an impartial jury of the State and district wherein the crime shall have been committed, which district shall have been previously ascertained by law, and to be informed of the nature and cause of the accusation; to be confronted with the witnesses against him; to have compulsory process for obtaining witnesses in his favor, and to have the Assistance of Counsel for his defense.

Amendment VII

In Suits at common law, where the value in controversy shall exceed twenty dollars, the right of trial by jury shall be preserved, and no fact tried by a jury, shall be otherwise re-examined in any Court of the United States, than according to the rules of the common law.

Amendment VIII

Excessive bail shall not be required, nor excessive fines imposed, nor cruel and unusual punishments inflicted.

Amendment IX

The enumeration in the Constitution, of certain rights, shall not be construed to deny or disparage others retained by the people.

Amendment X

The powers not delegated to the United States by the Constitution, nor prohibited by it to the States, are reserved to the States respectively, or to the people.

The Constitution: Amendments 11-27

Constitutional Amendments 1-10 make up what is known as The Bill of Rights.
Amendments 11-27 are listed below.

AMENDMENT XI

Passed by Congress March 4, 1794. Ratified February 7, 1795.

Note: Article III, section 2, of the Constitution was modified by amendment 11.

The Judicial power of the United States shall not be construed to extend to any suit in law or equity, commenced or prosecuted against one of the United States by Citizens of another State, or by Citizens or Subjects of any Foreign State.

AMENDMENT XII

Passed by Congress December 9, 1803. Ratified June 15, 1804.

Note: A portion of Article II, section 1 of the Constitution was superseded by the 12th amendment.

The Electors shall meet in their respective states and vote by ballot for President and Vice-President, one of whom, at least, shall not be an inhabitant of the same state with themselves; they shall name in their ballots the person voted for as President, and in distinct ballots the person voted for as Vice-President, and they shall make distinct lists of all persons voted for as President, and of all persons voted for as Vice-President, and of the number of votes for each, which lists they shall sign and certify, and transmit sealed to the seat of the government of the United States, directed to the President of the Senate; -- the President of the Senate shall, in the presence of the Senate and House of Representatives, open all the certificates and the votes shall then be counted; -- The person having the greatest number of votes for President, shall be the President, if such number be a majority of the whole number of Electors appointed; and if no person have such majority, then from the persons having the highest numbers not exceeding three on the list of those voted for as President, the House of Representatives shall choose immediately, by ballot, the President. But in choosing the President, the votes shall be taken by states, the representation from each state having one vote; a quorum for this purpose shall consist of a member or members from two-thirds of the states, and a majority of all the states shall be necessary to a choice. [And if the House of Representatives shall not choose a President whenever the right of choice shall devolve upon them, before the

148

fourth day of March next following, then the Vice-President shall act as President, as in case of the death or other constitutional disability of the President. --]* The person having the greatest number of votes as Vice-President, shall be the Vice-President, if such number be a majority of the whole number of Electors appointed, and if no person have a majority, then from the two highest numbers on the list, the Senate shall choose the Vice-President; a quorum for the purpose shall consist of two-thirds of the whole number of Senators, and a majority of the whole number shall be necessary to a choice. But no person constitutionally ineligible to the office of President shall be eligible to that of Vice-President of the United States.

*Superseded by section 3 of the 20th amendment.

AMENDMENT XIII

Passed by Congress January 31, 1865. Ratified December 6, 1865.

Note: A portion of Article IV, section 2, of the Constitution was superseded by the 13th amendment.

Section 1.

Neither slavery nor involuntary servitude, except as a punishment for crime whereof the party shall have been duly convicted, shall exist within the United States, or any place subject to their jurisdiction.

Section 2.

Congress shall have power to enforce this article by appropriate legislation.

AMENDMENT XIV

Passed by Congress June 13, 1866. Ratified July 9, 1868.

Note: Article I, section 2, of the Constitution was modified by section 2 of the 14th amendment.

Section 1.

All persons born or naturalized in the United States, and subject to the jurisdiction thereof, are citizens of the United States and of the State wherein they reside. No State shall make or enforce any law which shall abridge the privileges or immunities of citizens of the United States; nor shall any State deprive any person of life, liberty, or property, without due process of law; nor deny to any person within its jurisdiction the equal protection of the laws.

Section 2.

Representatives shall be apportioned among the several States according to their respective numbers, counting the whole number of persons in each State, excluding Indians not taxed. But when the right to vote at any election for the choice of electors for President and Vice-President of the United States, Representatives in Congress, the Executive and Judicial officers of a State, or the members of the Legislature thereof, is denied to any of the male inhabitants of such State, being twenty-one years of age,* and citizens of the United States, or in any way abridged, except for participation in rebellion, or other crime, the basis of representation therein shall be reduced in the proportion which the number of such male citizens shall bear to the whole number of male citizens twenty-one years of age in such State.

Section 3.

No person shall be a Senator or Representative in Congress, or elector of President and Vice-President, or hold any office, civil or military, under the United States, or under any State, who, having previously taken an oath, as a member of Congress, or as an officer of the United States, or as a member of any State legislature, or as an executive or judicial officer of any State, to support the Constitution of the United States, shall have engaged in insurrection or rebellion against the same, or given aid or comfort to the enemies thereof. But Congress may by a vote of two-thirds of each House, remove such disability.

Section 4.

The validity of the public debt of the United States, authorized by law, including debts incurred for payment of pensions and bounties for services in suppressing insurrection or rebellion, shall not be questioned. But neither the United States nor any State shall assume or pay any debt or obligation incurred in aid of insurrection or rebellion against the United States, or any claim for the loss or emancipation of any slave; but all such debts, obligations and claims shall be held illegal and void.

Section 5.

The Congress shall have the power to enforce, by appropriate legislation, the provisions of this article.

*Changed by section 1 of the 26th amendment.

AMENDMENT XV

Passed by Congress February 26, 1869. Ratified February 3, 1870.

Section 1.

The right of citizens of the United States to vote shall not be denied or abridged by the United States or by any State on account of race, color, or previous condition of servitude--

Section 2.

The Congress shall have the power to enforce this article by appropriate legislation.

AMENDMENT XVI

Passed by Congress July 2, 1909. Ratified February 3, 1913.

Note: Article I, section 9, of the Constitution was modified by amendment 16.

The Congress shall have power to lay and collect taxes on incomes, from whatever source derived, without apportionment among the several States, and without regard to any census or enumeration.

AMENDMENT XVII

Passed by Congress May 13, 1912. Ratified April 8, 1913.

Note: Article I, section 3, of the Constitution was modified by the 17th amendment.

The Senate of the United States shall be composed of two Senators from each State, elected by the people thereof, for six years; and each Senator shall have one vote. The electors in each State shall have the qualifications requisite for electors of the most numerous branch of the State legislatures.

When vacancies happen in the representation of any State in the Senate, the executive authority of such State shall issue writs of election to fill such vacancies: *Provided*, That the legislature of any State may empower the executive thereof to make temporary appointments until the people fill the vacancies by election as the legislature may direct.

This amendment shall not be so construed as to affect the election or term of any Senator chosen before it becomes valid as part of the Constitution.

AMENDMENT XVIII

Passed by Congress December 18, 1917. Ratified January 16, 1919. Repealed by amendment 21.

Section 1.

After one year from the ratification of this article the manufacture, sale, or transportation of intoxicating liquors within, the importation thereof into, or the exportation thereof from the United States and all territory subject to the jurisdiction thereof for beverage purposes is hereby prohibited.

Section 2.

The Congress and the several States shall have concurrent power to enforce this article by appropriate legislation.

Section 3.

This article shall be inoperative unless it shall have been ratified as an amendment to the Constitution by the legislatures of the several States, as provided in the Constitution, within seven years from the date of the submission hereof to the States by the Congress.

AMENDMENT XIX

Passed by Congress June 4, 1919. Ratified August 18, 1920.

The right of citizens of the United States to vote shall not be denied or abridged by the United States or by any State on account of sex.

Congress shall have power to enforce this article by appropriate legislation.

AMENDMENT XX

Passed by Congress March 2, 1932. Ratified January 23, 1933.

Note: Article I, section 4, of the Constitution was modified by section 2 of this amendment. In addition, a portion of the 12th amendment was superseded by section 3.

Section 1.

The terms of the President and the Vice President shall end at noon on the 20th day of January, and the terms of Senators and Representatives at noon on the 3d day of January, of the years in which such terms would have ended if this article had not been ratified; and the terms of their successors shall then begin.

Section 2.

The Congress shall assemble at least once in every year, and such meeting shall begin at noon on the 3d day of January, unless they shall by law appoint a different day.

Section 3.

If, at the time fixed for the beginning of the term of the President, the President elect shall have died, the Vice President elect shall become President. If a President shall not have been chosen before the time fixed for the beginning of his term, or if the President elect shall have failed to qualify, then the Vice President elect shall act as President until a President shall have qualified; and the Congress may by law provide for the case wherein neither a President elect nor a Vice President shall have qualified, declaring who shall then act as

President, or the manner in which one who is to act shall be selected, and such person shall act accordingly until a President or Vice President shall have qualified.

Section 4.

The Congress may by law provide for the case of the death of any of the persons from whom the House of Representatives may choose a President whenever the right of choice shall have devolved upon them, and for the case of the death of any of the persons from whom the Senate may choose a Vice President whenever the right of choice shall have devolved upon them.

Section 5.

Sections 1 and 2 shall take effect on the 15th day of October following the ratification of this article.

Section 6.

This article shall be inoperative unless it shall have been ratified as an amendment to the Constitution by the legislatures of three-fourths of the several States within seven years from the date of its submission.

AMENDMENT XXI

Passed by Congress February 20, 1933. Ratified December 5, 1933.

Section 1.

The eighteenth article of amendment to the Constitution of the United States is hereby repealed.

Section 2.

The transportation or importation into any State, Territory, or Possession of the United States for delivery or use therein of intoxicating liquors, in violation of the laws thereof, is hereby prohibited.

Section 3.

This article shall be inoperative unless it shall have been ratified as an amendment to the Constitution by conventions in the several States, as provided in the Constitution, within seven years from the date of the submission hereof to the States by the Congress.

AMENDMENT XXII

Passed by Congress March 21, 1947. Ratified February 27, 1951.

Section 1.

No person shall be elected to the office of the President more than twice, and no person who has held the office of President, or acted as President, for more than two years of a term to which some other person was elected President shall be elected to the office of President more than once. But this Article shall not apply to any person holding the office of President when this Article was proposed by Congress, and shall not prevent any person who may be holding the office of President, or acting as President, during the term within which this Article becomes operative from holding the office of President or acting as President during the remainder of such term.

Section 2.

This article shall be inoperative unless it shall have been ratified as an amendment to the Constitution by the legislatures of three-fourths of the several States within seven years from the date of its submission to the States by the Congress.

AMENDMENT XXIII

Passed by Congress June 16, 1960. Ratified March 29, 1961.

Section 1.

The District constituting the seat of Government of the United States shall appoint in such manner as Congress may direct:

A number of electors of President and Vice President equal to the whole number of Senators and Representatives in Congress to which the District would be entitled if it were a State, but in no event more than the least populous State; they shall be in addition to those appointed by the States, but they shall be considered, for the purposes of the election of President and Vice President, to be electors appointed by a State; and they shall meet in the District and perform such duties as provided by the twelfth article of amendment.

Section 2.

The Congress shall have power to enforce this article by appropriate legislation.

AMENDMENT XXIV

Passed by Congress August 27, 1962. Ratified January 23, 1964.

Section 1.

The right of citizens of the United States to vote in any primary or other election for President or Vice President, for electors for President or Vice President, or for Senator or Representative in Congress, shall not be denied or abridged by the United States or any State by reason of failure to pay poll tax or other tax.

Section 2.

The Congress shall have power to enforce this article by appropriate legislation.

AMENDMENT XXV

Passed by Congress July 6, 1965. Ratified February 10, 1967.

Note: Article II, section 1, of the Constitution was affected by the 25th amendment.

Section 1.

In case of the removal of the President from office or of his death or resignation, the Vice President shall become President.

Section 2.

Whenever there is a vacancy in the office of the Vice President, the President shall nominate a Vice President who shall take office upon confirmation by a majority vote of both Houses of Congress.

Section 3.

Whenever the President transmits to the President pro tempore of the Senate and the Speaker of the House of Representatives his written declaration that he is unable to discharge the powers and duties of his office, and until he transmits to them a written declaration to the contrary, such powers and duties shall be discharged by the Vice President as Acting President.

Section 4.

Whenever the Vice President and a majority of either the principal officers of the executive departments or of such other body as Congress may by law provide, transmit to the President pro tempore of the Senate and the Speaker of the House of Representatives their written declaration that the President is unable to discharge the powers and duties of his office, the Vice President shall immediately assume the powers and duties of the office as Acting President.

Thereafter, when the President transmits to the President pro tempore of the Senate and the Speaker of the House of Representatives his written declaration that no inability exists, he shall resume the powers and duties of his office unless the Vice President and a majority of either the principal officers of the executive department or of such other body as Congress may by law provide, transmit within four days to the President pro tempore of the Senate and the Speaker of the House of

Representatives their written declaration that the President is unable to discharge the powers and duties of his office. Thereupon Congress shall decide the issue, assembling within forty-eight hours for that purpose if not in session. If the Congress, within twenty-one days after receipt of the latter written declaration, or, if Congress is not in session, within twenty-one days after Congress is required to assemble, determines by two-thirds vote of both Houses that the President is unable to discharge the powers and duties of his office, the Vice President shall continue to discharge the same as Acting President; otherwise, the President shall resume the powers and duties of his office.

AMENDMENT XXVI

Passed by Congress March 23, 1971. Ratified July 1, 1971.

Note: Amendment 14, section 2, of the Constitution was modified by section 1 of the 26th amendment.

Section 1.

The right of citizens of the United States, who are eighteen years of age or older, to vote shall not be denied or abridged by the United States or by any State on account of age.

Section 2.

The Congress shall have power to enforce this article by appropriate legislation.

AMENDMENT XXVII

Originally proposed <u>Sept. 25, 1789</u>. Ratified May 7, 1992.

No law, varying the compensation for the services of the Senators and Representatives, shall take effect, until an election of representatives shall have intervened.